D0233044

On the Social Utility
of Psychopathology

On the Social Utility of Psychopathology

A Deviant Majority and Its Keepers?

Nathaniel J. Pallone

With a foreword by Ivan Illich

Transaction Books
New Brunswick (U.S.A.) and Oxford (U.K.)

Library of Congress Catalog Number: 85-983
ISBN 0-88738-048-4 (cloth)
Printed in the United States of America

Library of Congress Cataloging in Publication Data

Pallone, Nathaniel J.
  On the social utility of psychopathology.

  Bibliography: p.
  Includes Index.
  1. Psychiatry—Methodology. 2. Psychology,
Pathological—Methodology. 3. Psychotherapy—Social
aspects. 4. Mental illness—Social aspects. I. Title.
RC437.5.P35   1986   362.2′042   85-983
ISBN 0-88738-048-4

For Letitia,
who awakened me to dream again

Contents

Foreword

Ivan Illich

When I pick up the week's mail, I am in the habit of settling in a fonda on a side street to sort out unsolicited weight. So it was that I first opened this manuscript; I turned haphazardly to a passage having to do with the Middle Ages—and began to squirm. No matter, however, that there were some details on the Benedictines in Salerno or the Church and the Sabbath to quibble about; the illustration makes Pallone's argument crystal clear. Dis-ease in our society is unlike dis-ease in any previous culture: Our society provides enormous pressure to provide care for dis-ease and to submit dis-ease to care.

Cultures, I believe, can be viewed as programs that offer their members symbols, motives, rules, and procedures that do two things: They alleviate pain and they strengthen the ability to suffer dis-ease. Our society has the opposite orientation. It proposes to kill pain and to treat dis-ease. By making of dis-ease a burden to be borne, every tradition in its own way has made dis-ease something to be suffered. Our society, by its insistence on treatment, has been the first to make dis-ease unbearable. Al Rhazi, the great Baghdad physician of the ninth century, seems to have known this: "The only pain that is unbearable is that which is experienced as treatable." The burden of dealing with dis-ease has now been shifted from the person who suffers it to the society that treats it. As Pallone shows, as a logical result treatment makes the person more similar to his therapist; no more suffering, but collaboration with the therapist, is the new answer to dis-ease.

What surprised me in this manuscript is the stark simplicity with which Pallone constructs his argument. First, he sums up the evidence for the two points that apply to all psychotherapeutic praxis: First, that the relief of psychopathological dis-ease is in no dependable way associated with psychotherapeutic treatment; and, second, that in all the schools of psychotherapy the only clear-cut criterion for terminating treatment is the limit of the patient's financial resources. But then Pallone becomes nasty and goes beyond anyone whom I have so far read or heard. He focuses on the divergent end-points that the three major families of psychotherapy propose as targets. And from his argument it becomes clear that what for one school represents success might, for the others, constitute that symptom which calls for the start of treatment; what is one party's success is for the others the diagnosis that calls for treatment. Counting on the pull of the troika, society acquires the license to create unlimited dis-ease, to define this dis-ease as intolerable by financing armies of dis-ease-alleviators, and yet remains free, providing "treatments" that are in even more profound contradiction with each other than were the religions of old.

I wish I had understood this long ago. I tried and did not understand when I wrote *Medical Nemesis*. Pallone's book is written for those of his colleagues who are as candidly self-critical as he; but its form should not discourage the growing minority of dropouts from "care" to follow his arguments when they want to "unplug" further.

Preface

Genuinely effective people-helping through professional psychotherapy has long seemed to me to require more than helping people.
Among other things, effective people-helping requires that the
people-helper help the help-seeker (or he or she upon whom help is
thrust) not merely to assess himself or herself intrapsychically but also
in relation to the society in which both helper and help-seeker live,
move, and have their being. Such assessment may indicate that, to effect significant improvement in the condition of the help-seeker,
change is required in the psychological self of the help-seeker *or* in the
society, in neither, or in both. But attention solely to the prospect or
the process of change in the self of the help-seeker under the assumption of stasis in the society constitutes mere people-fitting. I am aware
that this sentiment may owe more to Vincent de Paul than to those personal heroes of mine who are adulated in this manuscript; but where
Illich and Schofield and even Laing and Szasz lead, there Vincent already stood, adamant in his insistence that people-helping alone, di-
vorced from a simultaneous assault on the structure of a society that
makes people-helping necessary, insults at once helper, helped, and
the society itself.

This manuscript had its origins during a semester I spent as a Hill
Foundation Visiting Professor at the University of Minnesota's Duluth
campus. After years of fairly traditional academic research, writing,
and clinical work, I found myself with the general assignment only to

"think large thoughts" and to share those that seemed worth sharing with faculty, students, and members of the professional community in three public lectures and a series of informal seminars. My research and clinical work then, as now, focused on the psychological treatment of criminal offenders—a group with the dubious distinction of dual deviance. But, as I reviewed the then-current issues in this specific field of application for therapeutic psychology within the general conceptual framework in which I had operated and which I had attempted to convey to my own graduate students at my home institution, I found that the conceptual issues that invited the thinking of large thoughts were, not surprisingly, those centered on the very notion of deviance: Why does society in some eras regard some behaviors as criminal, but not in others? Why does society in some eras regard some behaviors as psychopathological, but not in others? What overarching principles, if any, seem to guide the demarcation of some behaviors as deviant in one way, but not the other? What overarching principles, if any, seem to underlie the societal function of organized efforts to "treat" people whose behavior is judged deviant?

Graduate students who had elected a career in one or the other of the so-called contemporary helping professions, principally psychology, social work, and psychiatry, found the "large" thoughts I preferred them during that period both engaging and disturbing, not infrequently concluding that those "large" thoughts constituted a sort of metaphysical joke, the more so since I framed them aphoristically in the effort to provide visible sparks at the initiation of each informal, maieutically-intended seminar; few of us, I suspect, like to see ourselves as society's gate-keepers when we believe we are motivated only by the highest concern for our fellows, nor as responding to arbitrarily designated categories of behavior in our professional people-helping. Yet a jaundiced skepticism about ourselves and our roles, I would argue, serves both ourselves, the help-seekers, and the society of which we are a part better than blind and canonical conviction; to paraphrase shamelessly, the unexamined people-helping profession is not worth practicing.

Upon return to Rutgers, I began to share with students and colleagues there the aphorisms, vignettes, and other maieutic devices I had employed in Duluth. To my surprise, they responded even more positively than they had to the more traditional, sterilely scientific exposition in which I had attempted to convey some of these same points in other lectures and writings; thus the manuscript germinated.

I have shared this manuscript in various drafts with many colleagues and friends, from whose harsh reading and criticism I hope I have profited. I am particularly grateful to Karl vander Horck, now emeritus at Minnesota, James Hennessy of Fordham, Robert Woolfolk and Milton Schwebel at Rutgers, Donald Biggs and James Mancuso of the State University of New York at Albany, and William Schofield of the University of Minnesota Medical School for their incisive observations. Jane Gottfried, Sally Cafasso, and Mary Westburg of the administrative staff at Rutgers provided not only invaluable assistance in completing the manuscript but a variety of other types of support, for which I remain in their debt.

N.P.

1

Of Schofield's Hyphen and Conceptual Landscapes

That encyclopedic nosology of mental illness, the *Diagnostic and Statistical Manual* of the American Psychiatric Association, enumerates some 165 distinct diagnostic categories for the classification of anomalies in thinking, feeling, and/or behaving that are discernible among adults.[1] Of these, 85 either originate in somatic processes or implicate somatic processes in their consequences. This group of disorders, which have either genesis or sequelae in physical pathology, are sometimes construed as demarking the arena of psychiatric pathology, while the remaining 80 diagnostic categories are construed as representing the arena of psychological pathologies, psychogenic in their origin and independent of somatic processes even in their consequences.

The group here syllabicated as the psychiatric pathologies includes a spectrum of relatively readily identifiable disorders ranging from senile dementia, activated by the inexorable effects of physical aging on the functioning of the brain, through opiate addiction, which may originate in a complex matrix of psychogenic factors but which results in effects on the central nervous system clearly discernible through medical examination. In contrast, the psychological pathologies denote a spectrum of conditions that range from zoophilia through kleptomania to a fierce and unbending preference for social isolation over the "togetherness" that has become a popular American ideal. Each such psychologically pathological condition is denominated by a five-digit

1

nosological code number of enormous value, recognized by psychological, psychiatric, and medical practitioners worldwide, on the basis of which the person identified as suffering the condition becomes admissible to professional treatment as an in-patient or as an out-patient and on the basis of which third-party medical insurance carriers can be required to provide the costs of such treatment.

There are few human conditions—including, indeed, a singular devotion to coffee or tobacco—that are free from the omnipresent five-digit code.

In a slim, provocative volume entitled *Psychotherapy: The Purchase of Friendship*, which deserves to be far better known to the clinician and general reader alike, Schofield inserts a hyphen into a familiar term in such a way as to effect a radical reconceptualization in its meaning: it becomes *psychological dis-ease*.[2]

Once Schofield's Hyphen has been inserted, the term denotes the subjective experience of psychological discomfort, which may or may not accompany an otherwise discernible psychological pathology and which may or may not be triggered by psychiatric pathology that originates in, or implicates, somatic processes. Indeed, in the marvelously circular and closed world of psychodiagnosis, the very failure to experience psychological dis-ease in the face of palpable psychiatric or psychological disorder is held to constitute a form of psychopathology itself.

But it is the subjective experience of discomfort that represents the focus for every contemporary school of psychotherapeutic theory and practice; whether the term is translated as "anxiety," "incongruence," or the simpler "motivation," virtually every school posits subjective dis-ease, the experience of a disorder as alien to the self or the experience of discomfort even in the absence of an otherwise recognizable disorder, as necessary to engage the psychotherapeutic transaction.[3] For those persons who evince either psychiatric or psychological disorder without simultaneously experiencing psychological dis-ease, the appropriate "treatment" may be another form of psychological, psychiatric, psychopharmocological, or even neurosurgical intervention—but not psychotherapy.

It is with the psychological disorders, whether accompanied by psychological dis-ease or not, and their treatment that this essay concerns itself; on psychiatric disorders, those anomalies in thinking, feeling, and behaving that involve somatic processes in their genesis or their sequlae, it remains largely silent.

It is the burden of this essay that, whatever else is true of psychopathology, such pathology serves purposes that are socially useful; that whatever else is true of its clinical treatment, such treatment functions as a form of societal regulation; that, in societal terms, such treatment may serve purposes quite other than the relief of psychological dis-ease or even the remedy of psychopathological disorder; that, indeed, if psychopathology failed to emerge as a naturally occurring phenomenon, society might need to engender psychopathogenic conditions both to fulfill socially useful purposes and to elicit that subtle mechanism for societal regulation we term psychotherapy.

As one gauges the sweep of human history, only within the relatively recent past has psychiatry emerged as a speciality within medicine; and, even more recently, and somewhat grudgingly at that, has psychotherapy been recognized as an enterprise distinct from psychiatry, practiced not only by physicians but also by a large and growing cadre of "human service workers" under an amazing variety of occupational titles.

Though psychiatry may seem currently in jeopardy of displacement as the primary source of "treatment" for conditions labelled psychopathological, the suzerainty of medicine in the way psychopathology has been construed conceptually and treated clinically itself owns but a short and erratic past.

Through much of recorded history, the genesis of psychopathology was attributed to powers external and perhaps supernatural, so that the dominant modes for its treatment became the invocation of successively stronger magic, first by shaman, then by priest, through the uttering of incantations, the prescribing of amulets, and ultimately the expulsion of evil spirits.[4]

For but a brief period in the ancient world, more consistently through the history of Islam, but firmly in the West only after the Renaissance, was the clinical treatment of psychopathology liberated from theological control to find more benign shelter under the mantle of medicine, with a radical shift in the undergirding conceptual construction of genesis and remedy from other-worldly to this-worldly, from the supernatural to the physiological. Only since Freud's time, scarcely a century ago and but a very minor part of the 10,000 years of recorded human history, have genesis and remedy been widely construed as intrapsychic and psychosocial.

And inevitably one era's magic evolves into another's science; the altar yields to the analyst's couch; the leeching of humors is succeeded by electroconvulsion; ritual prayer gives way to verbal conditioning; portable, self-administered biofeedback gadgets descend linearly from amulets; encounter weekends recall the "ships of fools" of the early Renaissance, which carried the psychologically disordered on a constant journey from port to port with no home mooring.[5] What perdures is the aura of conjuring, clearly visible in the processes adopted for clinical "treatment" in one era and the next but discernible as well in the ways in which one era and the next construes the genesis of psychopathology.

With the ascendance since Freud's time of the yet more radical construction that psychopathology arises from intrapsychic and psychosocial sources, as Bromberg[6] has it, psychotherapy broadened from a medical specialty to a panoply of new forms of non-medical treatment for "patients" whose somatic processes are neither impaired nor implicated in disordered mental or emotional processes, but who nonetheless evince distortions in their behavior sufficient to engender the subjective experience of dis-ease and/or to interfere with their psychological functioning in ways so obvious that others societally empowered to make such judgments regard their behavior as "pathological" or "abnormal."

With so large and expansive a cadre of people-helpers engaged in the campaign to alleviate psychopathological disorder, one might expect to find the mental health of the nation at an all-time high. Not so, if we are to believe the studies of such epidemiologists as Leo Srole and his successors, whose results consistently indicate, whether in U.S. cities or in rural Canada, that alarmingly high proportions of the general population are so dis-eased or disordered psychologically as to require professional care, or, more frighteningly, that very small proportions of the population (in most cases, no higher than 20 percent) are free of psychopathological symptoms,[7] and that only this latter group are not entitled, each and severally, to be denominated by one or another five-digit code. To paraphrase Martinson[8] in another context, how can it be that all the well-intentioned efforts of the psychiatric, psychological, and social service communities, of the medical establishment, of the prisons and the jails, and even of the schools have yielded such disappointing results? Can it be that, while one set of forces propels our humanely-caring society to provide dis-ease-alleviating services on an unprecedented scale, another set of forces engenders psychopathological dis-ease on an unprecedented scale? Or, even more perversely, that the same set of forces both engenders disease and propels the commissioning of an army of people-helpers and dis-ease-alleviators?

To have endured through successive epochs of nascent and burgeoning empiricism in science and medicine, the attribution of psychopathology to extranatural forces must have been supported by strong elements within the structure of several successive societies, must have served purposes useful not merely in a single and perhaps aberrant society, but in a succession of societies, each organized around distinct but discernible sets of first premises. And it may be that our contemporary approaches to psychopathology and its treatment, to say nothing of the explosion in the "human service" professions, may serve similarly useful purposes in a society anchored in yet other premises.

If we inspect several propositional vignettes, broadly sketched in the manner of minimalist cinema and frankly intended as evocative rather than as definitive, portraying how psychopathology was construed and treated in ancient and medieval cultures, and how it is construed and treated in our own, might we discern what socially useful purposes psychopathology and its treatment held in those societies, or holds for us today? Might we discern the value psychopathology yields in the organization, integration, or cohesion of a society?

Clearly one never embarks on such a quest without biases and preconceptions; thus candor alone requires that one posit, however provisionally, his prime assumptions: That those values that a society holds most tenaciously are those that are essential to its continued existence, and that those values will be discernible both in the conception of the "good life" held by a society and in the structure of the formal institutions that a society establishes to regulate and to perpetuate itself.

If it be the case that the ways in which psychopathology has been, and is, construed and treated are in at least some measure socially determined and governed, that they respond to forces inherent in the social fabric, then we might find that a society's essential values and its conception of the "good life" are reflected in the ways in which psychopathology is construed and in the dominant methods each society devises and supports for its treatment. We might indeed discern how psychopathology functions as a societal institution and how those who are identified as psychopathologically disordered themselves play societally defined roles useful to the maintenance of the social fabric.

Notes

1. American Psychiatric Association, *Diagnostic and Statistical Manual of Mental Disorders*, 3d ed.(Washington, D.C.: American Psychiatric Association, 1980). The *Manual* also enumerates some 45 diagnostic categories for children and adolescents, of which 15 represent psychiatric disorders.

2. See William Schofield, *Psychotherapy: The Purchase of Friendship* (Englewood Cliffs, N.J.: Prentice-Hall, 1964), pp. 17-23.

3. Most typically, the subjective experience of psychological dis-ease is encapsulated by the quasi-technical term "anxiety," the detection of which in itself is sufficient to categorize the dis-eased by means of a five-digit code, sometimes "secondary" to some other five-digit condition. Schofield (*Psychotherapy: The Purchase of Friendship,* pp. 43-44), however, comments trenchantly that "Anxiety . . . is no more pathological than hope— but our present culture has chosen to be anxious about anxiety."

4. See Walter Bromberg, *The Mind of Man: A History of Psychotherapy and Psychoanalysis* (New York: Harper & Row, 1963); *idem, From Shaman to Psychotherapist: A History of the Treatment of Mental Illness* (Chicago: Henry Regenry, 1975). Richard Bandler and John Grinder's *The Structure of Magic* (Palo Alto: Science & Behavior Books, 1975) is also instructive.

5. See Michel Foucault, *Madness and Civilization: A History of Insanity in the Age of Reason* (New York: Random House, 1965), pp. 3-37.

6. Bromberg, *The Mind of Man*, pp. 6-7.

7. Epidemiological studies of the general population find psychological dis-ease at a level of severity requiring professional intervention among 22 percent of those studied (with only 19 percent entirely symptom-free) in the famous midtown Manhattan survey by Leo Srole, Thomas S. Langer, Stanley T. Michael, Marvin K. Opler, and Thomas A.C. Bennie, *Mental Health in the Metropolis* (New York: McGraw-Hill, 1962), pp. 210-52; among 20 to 30 percent of those studied in rural towns in eastern Canada, again with only 19 percent symptom-free, by Dorothea C. Leighton, Alexander H. Leighton, and R.A. Armstrong, "Commu-

nity Psychiatry in a Rural Area: A Social Psychiatric Approach,'' in Leopold Bellak, ed., *Handbook of Community Psychiatry* (New York: Grune & Stratton, 1968), among 18 percent of those studied in New Haven by Myrna M. Weissman, Jerome K. Myers, and Pamela S. Harding, "Psychiatric Disorders in a U.S. Urban Community," *American Journal of Psychiatry* 135 (1978), 459-62; and among 40 percent of those studied in Chicago by Frederic W. Ilfeld, Jr., "Psychological Status of Community Residents along Major Demographic Dimensions," *Archives of General Psychiatry* 35 (1978), 716-24. John A. Clausen, Nancy G. Pfeffer, and Carol L. Huffine, "Help-Seeking in Severe Mental Illness," in David Mechanic, ed., *Symptoms, Illness Behavior, and Help-Seeking* (New York: Prodist/Neale Watson, 1982), pp. 135-155, review their own data and studies by others on the mechanisms through which the diseased seek psychiatric help. In commenting on the early findings of Srole and his associates, Schofield (*Psychotherapy: The Purchase of Friendship,* p. 13) opines that the incidence of psychological dis-ease increases during those periods in the national economy when we are affluent enough to afford the relative luxury of mental health census-taking.

8. Robert Martinson, "California Research at the Crossroads," *Crime and Delinquency* 14 (1976), 189-99.

2

The Eye of the Beholder

In the Persian Gulf a dozen miles off the coast of Saudi Arabia lies an archipelago known collectively as Bahrain. Its largest island measures but 30 miles at its width and 12 miles at its length; ruled as a hereditary Moslem sheikdom since the seventeenth century, the current population of the archipelago numbers fewer than 400,000.

Without overly romanticizing the history of this remote land, somewhat mysterious and little known in the West until petroleum deposits were discovered on the principal island in the chain some 60 years ago, the case can be made that Bahrain had changed little in three centuries. Indeed, as recently as 1950, bloody sacrifice was offered on Islamic holy days.

The economic life of the sheikdom began to shift after Standard Oil and Texaco arrived during the 1920s and 1930s, but major social change waited until the mid-1970's, when incessant civil strife rent the state of Lebanon. Beirut, its capital city, had long served as the commercial center of the Arab world and the Middle East generally. But guerilla warfare in the streets of that metropolis rendered the pursuit of commerce on an international scale there first tenuous, then impossible. Accordingly, Beirut's major banks began to transfer their operations to the tranquil island sheikdom in the Gulf.

With the banks came the trappings of Westernized commerce: other financial institutions, computer installations, luxury hotels.

And with the hotels, into this geographically isolated Moslem en-

8

clave, came the lubricants of Western commerce: fermented and distilled spirits.

According to a report by the chief psychiatrist in the sheikdom's only comprehensive mental hospital, the use, let alone the abuse, of alcohol had been virtually unknown among the people of Bahrain until the intrusion of the banks of Beirut. But now the erstwhile abstinent natives no longer so readily conform their wills to the dictates of the Koran; it has become almost commonplace that the porter in the luxury hotel who has pilfered his fill of Western booze permits his bicycle to careen carelessly into the rear end of a local bus, may Allah turn aside his face.

The response of the medical community has been both electric and informed by the commingling of East and West. In the space of a few short years, there have been established not only an alcoholism rehabilitation program but also a far-reaching regimen of education into the debilitating effects of the merest passing acquaintance with alcohol, both with a strong theological component.[1]

Booze in Bahrain and Boston; toplessness in Bali and Baltimore; polygamy in a remote village in Africa's Ruwenzori range or in Utah's Abajo.

For the sociologist Kai Erikson, "Deviance is not a property *inherent in* any particular kind of behavior; it is a property *conferred upon* that behavior by the people who come into contact with it"; hence, "deviance refers to conduct which the people of a group consider so dangerous or embarassing or irritating that they bring special sanctions to bear against the persons who exhibit it."[2]

Against such a conceptual backdrop, though they may address the *that* of it more persuasively than the *why* of it, some highly visible renegades in the contemporary sciences of psychiatry and psychology speak as if with one voice. Among the psychologists, Adams sets it forth that "when the term 'mental illness' is used and no organic pathology is in evidence, the term refers to some arbitrarily defined pattern of conduct,"[3] while Sarbin and Mancuso go him one better by explicitly pronouncing one category of mental illness (schizophrenia) "a moral verdict masquerading as a medical diagnosis"[4] and coming close to so characterizing all categories of psychological and psychiatric disorder. Among the psychiatrists, Laing, lately transformed into an obscurantist poet, declares that the standard psychiatric patient is a function of the standard psychiatrist;[5] and Szasz, jousting for the title champion iconoclast, stoutly insists that madness is a myth manufactured by the dis-ease-alleviators themselves.[6]

Laing and Szasz, Sarbin and Mancuso and their cohort of true non-believers seem to argue that we have built hospitals and community mental health centers and commissioned an army of professional and paraprofessional people-helpers to "treat" behavior that is merely embarrassing, irritating, or otherwise dis-accommodating, for no sounder reason than a set of motes in particular sets of eyes; that the legions of people-helpers and dis-ease-alleviators hew merely to socially relativistic standards; and that nowhere, it seems to follow, will we find in the lexicon of psychopathology analogues to those well-defined, non-overlapping patterns of symptoms, each replete with a discernible etiology and a predictable course, that characterize physical disease in the lexicon of medicine. Even a sober and traditional commentator like Achenbach complains of "the lack of accepted definitions for the [psychopathological] disorders themselves" and bridles that "few disorders have been operationally defined."[7]

So: Psychopathology, or at least that psychopathology which is observed independently of medically-identifiable physical pathology, is but a myth, say the iconoclasts and the sober-sides alike, a mote in the eye, lacking substance, a socially relativistic construct invented to denote merely that which the rest of us find odd or offensive.

How is it, then, that epidemiologists Plunkett and Gordon define physical health as "the achievement of a dominance of positive adaptations to the environment" and disease as "the dominance of negative or unfavorable adaptations"? [8]

Plunkett and Gordon's definitions veer quite far from the tidy notion of the package of symptoms with the predictable course, the discernible etiology, and all that; they employ little in the way of absolute standards but instead seem to suggest strongly relativistic perspectives. One need but interpose the modifier "psychosocial" before "environment" to render these definitions of physical health and illness equally serviceable to the Laing-Szasz heretical axis. One hears the echo of Illich's insistence that "All [physical] disease is but a socially created reality."[9]

Is one to conclude, then, that psychopathology is no *more* "real" than physical pathology?

Or no *less*?

Notes

1. Conditions in Bahrain were detailed at a symposium on the epidemiology of alcohol abuse in the Third World at the Fourth International Congress on Alcohol and Drug Dependence, Liverpool University, April 1978.
2. Kai T. Erikson, *Wayward Puritans: A Study in the Sociology of Deviance* (New York: Wiley, 1966), p. 6.
3. Henry Adams, "Mental Illness or Interpersonal Behavior?" *American Psychologist* 19 (1964), 19, 191-97.
4. Theodore R. Sarbin and James C. Mancuso, *Schizophrenia: Medical Diagnosis or Moral Verdict?* (New York: Pergamon, 1980), p. 220.
5. See especially Ronald D. Laing, *The Divided Self* (London: Tavistock, 1960); *Self and Others* (New York: Pantheon, 1969); and *The Politics of the Family* (New York: Pantheon, 1971). Laing's poetry is found in two volumes of "psychiatric" verse: *Knots* (New York: Pantheon, 1971), Do You Love Me? (New York: Pantheon, 1976).
6. Thomas S. Szasz, *Myth of Mental Illness* (New York: Harper & Row, 1961); *Law, Liberty, and Psychiatry* (New York: Collier, 1968); *The Manufacture of Madness* (New York: Harper & Row: 1970); *Psychiatric Slavery* (New York: Pantheon, 1978).
7. Thomas M. Achenbach, "What Is Child Psychiatric Epidemiology the Epidemiology Of?" in Felton Earls, ed., *Psychosocial Epidemiology: Studies of Children* (New York: Neale Watson Academic, 1980), pp. 96-116.
8. Richard J. Plunkett and John E. Gordon, *Epidemiology and Mental Illness* (New York: Basic Books, 1960), p. 10.
9. Ivan Illich, *Medical Nemesis: The Expropriation of Health* (London: Calder & Boyars, 1975), p. 117.

3

Whom the Gods Would Destroy

Our first vignette takes us to antique times. The specific formulation
may be Elizabethan, but the sentiment is much, much older; the theme
is to be found in the earliest cave art of prehistory and in the folk
medicine of the dawn of civilization.

One of the very earliest of the surviving medical papyrii of ancient
Egypt contains the "Book of the Heart," which dates from 1550 B.C.
In it, we learn that what is called "the perishing of the mind" is to be
attributed to a spell cast by a priest and that "raving" is to be attributed
to control of the raving person by members of the nether world. Similarly, epilepsy is attributed to spirit possession, with the spirit attached
in some ancient Egyptian medical texts to the stomach, in others to the
eyes. Epilepsy is to be treated with an externally applied unction con-
taining pork fat and the urine of a virgin.[1]

To put these observations in context: Many of the medical papyrii of
this period claim divine origin—that is, claim to be revealed truth; and
many prescribe the casting of spells or the uttering of incantations as
remedies, even of physical disorders attributed to natural physical
causes. This "white magic" seems to have as its purpose appeasing or
controlling the spirits who afflict the psychopathologically dis-eased;
there is no question, yet, of a formal ritual to drive the spirits away.

Cinematically, a slow "dissolve"—to Athens, in the fifth century B.C.
We'll find Plato composing the "Phaedrus," declaring therein that

there are two kinds of madness. One involves a mental strain that arises from the body, but the other is divine or inspired, with Apollo as the chief source of inspiration. And, in the Dialogues, Plato recommends treatment of madness by means of amulets and charms.[2]

Another slow dissolve. Now to Britain in the late tenth century A.D. "The Leech Book of Blad," a remarkable collection of medical prescriptions for diseases of all sorts, is newly ensconced in the monastery libraries of the land. It tells us: "When a devil possess a man or controls him from within, he is to be given an emetic, lupin, henbane, or corpleek"; these are to be "pounded together, add ale for a liquid, let it stand for a night, add fifty bibcorns of cathartic grains, and *Holy Water*." When this concoction has aged sufficiently, "have him drink the liquid *out of a church bell*."[3] Other texts of the time seem similarly to combine naturalistic therapies with religious acts, almost as if to hedge one's bets. For example, Roger of Salerno exhorts the surgeon who would release *either* the vile humors *or* the pressures *or* the demons responsible for "mania and melancholia" to "incise the top of the head *in the shape of a Cross* and perforate the cranium so as to expel the noxious matter."[4]

Psychological pathology is caused by spirits, perhaps by demons, but is treated through a mixture of natural and supernatural means, with the latter mild and essentially harmless. We are not surprised to find, in an era before the emergence of empirical science, that the unknown is attributed to the unseen as its cause. But there is as yet no widespread appeal to the ritual of exorcism, nor is the host for the demon himself pronounced evil.

Notes

1. Paul Ghalioungui, *The House of Life: Magic and Medical Science in Ancient Egypt* (Amsterdam: Israel, 1973), pp. 29-30, 127-28.
2. Charles E. Goshen, *A Documentary History of Psychiatry: A Source Book on Historical Principles* (New York: Philosophical Library, 1967), pp. 18-19.
3. Cited in Bromberg, *From Shaman to Psychotherapist*, p. 25.
4. Cited in Loren MacKinney, *Medical Illustrations in Medieval Manuscripts* (Berkeley: University of California Press, 1965), p. 69.

4

Naturalistic Psychiatry Is Born— and Dies

We move backward in time, to Greece in the fifth century before Christ. Hippocrates is to be found fathering medicine, in the process insisting that all diseases arise from natural, not supernatural, causes, and classifying mental illness according to some remarkably durable categories as epilepsy, phobia, mania, melancholia, and paranoia. But Hippocrates believes that it is the balance between humors (blood, phlegm, yellow bile, black bile) that determines health or illness, including mental health or illness.[1] There is little room in Hippocrates' thought for spirits, good or evil. Hippocrates' medical formulations survive, but his psychiatric formulations soon enough disappear from the West for almost a thousand years. Why?

Quickly to Rome in the second century A.D. Here we meet Galen, already known as a great physician, serving as surgeon to the Gladiators. Between bouts, he preserves the tradition of Hippocrates. Though his medical formulations remain influential, his notions on psychiatry, largely Hippocratic, also soon disappear.[2]

Next we sweep across sand dunes; these might suggest both the passage of time and the deserts of North Africa. Briefly we glimpse the visage of Nestorius, one of the great Desert Fathers, a Syrian monk who became Patriarch of Constantinople in 428 A.D. but who, with his followers and their books—and their books included copies of the texts

14

of Hippocrates and Galen, perhaps the only copies not purged of what the Christian church came to regard as theological error—was banished to North Africa in consequence of his heresies arguing the dual nature of Christ, formally condemned at the Third Council of Ephesus. His heretical followers eventually founded medical schools in Mesopotamia and in Persia, where they flourished under Arabian protection. And they translated into Syrian and then into Arabic their copies of Hippocrates' original Greek texts and their Greek version of Galen's Latin texts.[3]

Rapid dissolve and fast forward. We are at the Benedictine Abbey at Monte Cassino near Salerno in Italy in the middle of the fourteenth century. We find the holy monks arming themselves with the weapons of war. Does the infidel threaten the serenity of their monastery? The surrounding contryside? No; they have been ordered to overrun the Benedictine Abbey at Salerno and there to bring to heel their fellow monks of the same rule and cloth, who have been declared ecclesiastical outlaws. Of what monstrous crimes are these Benedictines of Salerno guilty, that their very brothers have been set upon them in such a ferocious and antifraternal expedition?

Why, these renegade priests of Salerno have dissociated themselves from monastic medicine, involving themselves in Europe's first (and to this point the only) secular school of medicine, taken it upon themselves to practice "Moslem" medicine—to practice indeed according to the texts of Hippocrates and Galen, preserved by the followers of Nestorius and then by the followers of Mohammed, brought to Salerno by the merchants who sailed East from this Mediterranean port city and by returning Crusaders. And they practice according to the commentaries and codicils of Averroes and Avicenna, both Moslem infidels, and of Moses Maimonides, infidel of infidels, who confessed the Judaic faith but who lived and worked in the Moslem world. And in what important ways does Moslem medicine differ so radically from that practiced in Christian Europe? In one way perhaps more important than the rest—in its insistence, along with Hippocrates and Galen, that all disease, including disease of the mind, is attributable to natural causes and that therefore the invocation of spirits or demons to explain such disease, or even the customary genuflection to such otherworldly nostrums as the use of a church bell as a vessel for a cathartic or a surgical incision in the shape of a cross, is superfluous ritualism.

And so the monks of Monte Cassino lay siege to the Abbey at Salerno. The Abbey capitulates, and with the capitulation is eclipsed the medical school the Benedictines of Salerno had supported, an institution that "aroused the healing art from the decrepitude of half a millenium, infused new life into things and guarded as a Palladium the best traditions of ancient practice" and at which "under Arabic influence medicine is taught for the first time in the medieval period as a separate branch of science, in distinction to the Monastic medicine prevalent elsewhere"; it has been less than a hundred years since Frederick II had granted the college at Salerno the sole right to award an official medical diploma within the confines of the Holy Roman Empire.[4]

Contemporaneously, the Augustinian Arnold of Villanova of the medical school at Montpelier is tried for heresy for introducing Hippocratic principles into the treatment of mental illness; the Franciscan Pietro Abano of the medical faculty of Padua is posthumously tried for heresy, his body exhumed, and his bones burned in 1316 because he not only minimized spiritual principles in healing but denied the existence of the devil.[5] Even Thomas Aquinas, centuries later to be designated the official philosopher of Christendom, is forced to flee from Paris to Cologne because he has the temerity to refer to the pagan Aristotle as "*the* Philosopher," to the Moslem Avicenna as "*the* Commentator," and even to cite favorably that infidel of infidels, Maimonides.

Formal institutions are required to reflect the values no less than the ways of construing reality dominant in the societies they serve; renegades are not to be tolerated.

Notes

1. Franz G. Alexander and Sheldon T. Selesnick, *The History of Psychiatry: An Evaluation of Psychiatric Thought and Practice* (New York: Harper & Row), pp. 30-33.
2. Howard W. Haggard, *Mystery, Magic, and Medicine* (Garden City, N.Y.: Doubleday, 1933), pp. 28-48. See also "White Magic and Black" in Haggard, *Devils, Drugs, and Doctors* (New York: Blue Ribbon, 1929).

Though his formulations on the genesis of psychopathology followed Hippocrates, Galen's treatment methods displayed great inventiveness; indeed, one case history displays Galen's use of a technique that Viktor Frankl would today instantly identify as paradoxical intention.

3. Haggard, *Mystery, Magic, and Medicine*, p. 46.

4. See Donald Campbell, *Arabian Medicine and Its Influence in the Middle Ages* (London: Kegan, Paul, French, Trubner, 1926), p. 125. This account of the suppression of the Abbey at Salerno may owe more to the oral tradition of Salernitian religious circles than to verifiable historical fact. Indeed, many authors in the history of medicine regard the medical school at Salerno as pivotal in the development of medicine as a science independent of theology; see, for example, Charles and Dorothea Singer, "The Origin of the Medical School of Salerno, the First University," in *Essays on the History of Medicine*, ed. by Charles Singer and Henry E. Sigerist (Freeport: Books for Libraries Press, 1924), pp. 121-38, and Hastings Rashdall, *The Universities of Europe in the Middle Ages* (Oxford: Clarendon Press, 1936), pp. 75-86. The importance of the institution is generally held to derive from four factors: its foundation in the tenth century as a "secular corporation," supported to be sure by the Abbey (which had opened a hospital in the city a century earlier) but also by leagues of citizens and merchants, which distinguished it from the institutions directly controlled by the abbeys and monasteries; from the influence of Byzantine and Arabic medicine evident in its practices from the time of its foundation, attributed by John William Draper in his *History of the Conflict between Religion and Science* (New York: D. Appleton, 1875), p. 115., to Saracens who modeled the institution after the medical college at Cairo, when in Haggard's account (*Devils, Drugs, and Doctors*, p. 136) "its first instructors were mostly Jews from Arabia" through the tenure of figures like Constantinus Africanus on its faculty in the eleventh century; from the instruction in medical science, or at least in midwifery, accorded to women, very likely for the first time anywhere; and from the inventive method of instruction, which required students, long before the invention of printing but also before the simultaneous copying of manuscripts read by a lector to several scribes became a cottage industry in the great monasteries, to memorize the principles of medical science and practice through an ever-accreting set of verses that initially numbered some 362 at the time of its foundation to more than 7,000 at the last printing in the mid-nineteenth century. By 1231, the school had established itself so thoroughly as a center for empirical medicine that Frederick II forbade the practice or teaching of medicine without a Royal License that could be conferred only by the faculty of the school at Salerno. That the medical school at Salerno declined in importance after the thirteenth century until it was ordered closed by Napoleon in 1811 is the general consensus, but the underlying reasons set forth vary widely. Similarly, the traditional account that the Abbey at Salerno was briefly suppressed by the monks of the larger and much more powerful Abbey at Monte Cassino as preserved in

legend seems probable; but such occurrences were by no means unique, and it may be no more than romantic legend that links these two, now quite distant, chains of events. Attempts at verification in the history of the Benedictines proves largely fruitless. As Fielding Garrison observes in *An Introduction to the History of Medicine* (Philadelphia: W.B. Saunders, 1924), p. 137, "there is significant silence about Salerno in the ecclesiastical chronicles." An alternate hypothesis, barely sketched by Rashdall, might root the conflict between the abbeys not only in their discrepant size and influence but also in conflicting temporal alliances, exacerbated by the fact that the Byzantine emperors long maintained suzerainty over the principality of Salerno, rather than in ideological differences about medical practices. Yet the account given here gains some credibility in the light of the Christian church's attitudes toward obstetrics and midwifery during the medieval period, when male physicians were categorically forbidden on theological grounds to attend at childbirth and various Church councils undertook to establish the rules of midwifery on the same grounds; indeed, Haggard (*Devils, Drugs, and Doctors*, p. 29) records the execution in 1522 of a Dr. Wett of Hamburg whose crime had been masquerading as a woman so that he might, as a physician, observe a childbirth the better to understand its anatomy and physiology.

5. Alexander and Selesnick, *The History of Psychiatry*, pp. 65-66; Campbell, *Arabian Medicine and Its Influence in the Middle Ages*, pp. 161-62.

5
Conjure the King of Darkness

With the atrocities practiced upon Frater Abano at Padua and Pere Villanova at Montpelier and the intimidation of the medical faculty at Salerno, the Christian church firmly asserted its dominion over the disorders and dis-eases of mind. As the distinguished psychoanalysts Franz Alexander and Sheldon Selesnick put it: "By and large, throughout the thirteenth and fourteenth centuries, the human body and its afflictions are dealt with by lay physicians, but the problems of the mind remain the domain of the clerical scholars."[1]

The stage was set for the beginning of one of the sorriest periods in human history, certainly the most inhumane in the history of the treatment of psychopathology, one that led to a trail of pyres across Europe, the British Isles, and the Americas and spanned a period of three centuries.

Now it was asserted that the psychopathologically disordered and dis-eased—those whose behavior was considered by others societally empowered to make such judgments as dangerous, irritating, or otherwise dis-accommodating—were not only at the mercy of extranatural forces, but that these extranatural forces were specifically demoniac; that those who were possessed by demons were not innocent victims of the power of Lucifer and his legions, as the authors of the New Testament seem to have Christ say,[2] but that they were rather the willing accomplices of the demon and thus the authors of their own disorder and/or dis-ease; and that therefore the appropriate "treatment" for psychopathological conditions lay not in the application of the methods of naturalistic medicine but in the powerful, supernatural method of exorcism. And if exorcism failed to effect cure, there was nothing for it but to destroy both demon and host, with incineration at the stake the method-of-choice for this last, most drastic form of "therapy."

The Egyptians, the Athenians, and earlier Christians had indeed, as we have seen, attributed psychopathology to extranatural causes, to possession—whether divine or demoniac. But rarely before had other than natural means, combined to be sure with some relatively harmless incantations or charms, been prescribed to rid the possessed of those forces, nor, in the main, had the possessed himself been regarded as the author of his own possession.

What events in the general cultural milieu triggered such extraordinary propositions? Rosen seems to argue that the verities of the church and the empire no longer sufficed to compensate for oppressive political, theological, economic, and social systems, and that indeed a mood of melancholy and foreboding hung over Christian Europe. As one commentator put it, during this period, "whether we read a chronicle, a poem, a sermon, or even a legal document, the same impression of sadness is produced by them all. A general sense of impending doom hung over men and women, aggravated by an obsession that the world was come to an end." [3]

Kai Erikson substantially agrees and further interprets the spread of belief in demoniac possession, in Satan's intervention in human affairs, and in willful consort with demons as a harbinger of the massive revolt against an over-organized society that came to flower in Luther's reformation but a few decades later. Though the notion of witchcraft, he observes, is "as old as history," the concept of a malevolent witch who rejects God to make a compact with Satan does not appear in Europe until late in the fourteenth century, so that "witchcraft was brought on the same current of change that introduced the Protestant Reformation. Perhaps no other form of crime in history has been a better index to social disruption and change, for outbreaks of witchcraft mania have generally taken place in societies which are experiencing a change of boundaries." [4]

Among the noble institutions gone corrupt in such an atmosphere were those of the Church itself. The once-reproachless monasteries had fallen into a sorry state indeed. In particular, though still recognized as an obligation imposed upon monks, priests, and nuns, the vow of celibacy lay open to challenge both intellectually and behaviorally. As the pastor of Loudon, Pere Urban Grandier, later wrote in his journal: "A promise to do the impossible is not binding. For the young male, [sexual] continence is impossible. Therefore no vow involving celibacy is binding." And further: "The priest does not embrace celibacy for the love of celibacy, but solely that he may be admitted to holy orders." Thus, his vow "does not proceed from his will, but is imposed upon him by the Church." Upon such premises, as Aldous Huxley renders it, it came to pass that "one midnight, in the echoing, empty church, Grandier as priest asked himself whether he took this woman to be his wedded wife and as bridegroom he answered in the affirmative. As priest, he invoked a blessing and as groom he knelt to receive it."[5]

The twelfth century had witnessed the spectacle of an Eloise and Abelard, whose romance, if Alexander and Selesnick are to be believed, constituted no more than child's play. "Townspeople often," they write, "sent prostitutes to the monasteries to protect the maidens of their villages. It became imperative to the church to launch an antierotic movement" designed to restore order within its own ranks.[6] The distinguished neo-Thomist Maritain echoes the observation, adding that, inevitably, the objects of the excesses of the monks and priests who elected to ignore the requirements of their vows were not infrequently nuns, themselves bound by similar vows and, one presumes, similarly longing for freedom therefrom: "Priests and regulars [i.e., members of the diocesan clergy as well as of the orders] many times exerted themselves, often in veritable gangs, to tear nuns from their cloisters and make them their 'wives.' Once the flight from the convent was accomplished, they came to unheard-of things; they held a sort of trade in profaned nuns; they veritably put them up for sale."[7]

It is difficult to conceive a set of conditions more conducive to eliciting a wholesale and widely shared projection, even at the expense of delusion. Celibacy is demanded of entrants into the religious life, then apparently the vow is widely ignored; the joys of the flesh clash more than occassionally with the guilt of the spirit. Some, like Grandier, are able to rationalize their guilt away; others require, in confor-

mance with an ancient script, a scapegoat capable of bearing their unbearable burden; in the event, the latter prevail.

According to Bromberg, the medieval theologians who wrestled
with the problem of restoring order to the monasteries and among the
clergy shared the obscene view that ''woman is a temple built over a
sewer filled with carnal lust.''[8] There is but a small step from that mi-
sogynic conviction to the projection that the burden of guilt for the
temptations and deeds of the flesh falls not at all upon errant priest or
monk but rather upon the women after whom they lusted. How account
for such compelling attractiveness, compelling enough to tempt to carnal sin those who are able to command bread and wine to transub-
stantiate into sacred flesh and blood? In the conceptual lexicon of the
era, there could be but one power on earth or beneath it: Enter the King
of Darkness.

Each of the great philosopher-theologians of the late middle ages
who are today revered as Fathers of the Church—St. Bonaventure, St.
Albert the Great, St. Thomas Aquinas—believed firmly in demons and
their capacity to control human behavior. Aquinas went so far as to as-
sert the possibility of sexual copulation between human beings and devils.[9] Thus, the projection is rationalized: The carnal temptations of a
celibate clergy arise from no internal failing; the woman carries the
demon, and willfully; for this reason, she is able to tempt to sin those
who have dedicated themselves to the imitation of Christ.

By the late fifteenth century, no less central a figure in Christendom
than the reigning pontiff himself had reason to know intimately—
though it is not recorded whether he had reason also to regret—the
temptations of the flesh that everywhere assaulted the cleric.

Giovanni Battista Cibo, cardinal-archbishop of Santa Cecilia, selected
the name Innocent VIII upon his accession to the throne of Peter.
Shortly thereafter, as Kuhner records it, ''Innocent showed to what
lengths depravity and the lack of all sense of dignity and seemliness
had gone when he held a magnificent wedding feast in the Vatican, on
the marriage of his depraved bastard son Franceschetto with Mad-
dalena de Medici, the daughter of Lorenzo II Magnifico,'' after which
''Franceschetto took up his residence in the Vatican in his capacity as
the Pope's official son.''[10]

Between preparing for a new Crusade against Islam and stifling the efforts of Cardinal della Mirandola to convene a world congress of philosophers and theologians of all faiths devoted to the dignity of the human person, Innocent VIII—whether through the psychological mechanism of reaction-formation, in harmony with a route to expiation through projection, or for reasons not recorded—fell under the sway of "two fanatical German Dominicans," Henry Kramer and James Sprenger, who were convinced that they had been inspired to cleanse Christendom of that corruption of soul and body so well illustrated by the personal life of the incumbent Successor to Peter himself.

And so it came to pass, in the Year of the Lord 1484, that His Holiness Innocent VIII was led to declare open war upon Satan and his minions in a papal Bull entitled Summis Desiderantes, in which the pontiff decried: "It has come to our ears, not without inflicting us with bitter sorrow, that many persons of both sexes, unmindful of their own salvation and straying from the Catholic faith, have abandoned themselves to evil incantations, spells, conjurations, and other accursed charms and crafts, enormities and horrid offenses. . . "

And in which the Vicar of Christ gave carte blanche to an unholy reign of terror: "Our dear sons, Henry Kramer and James Sprenger, professors of theology of the Order of Friars Preachers, have been by these Letters Apostolic designated as Inquisitors of these heretical pravities."[11]

Kramer and Sprenger proved more than equal to their awesome task. To guide themselves and an army of deputies in this new Crusade, they composed the infamous Witches' Hammer, described by Alexander and Selesnick as simultaneously an encylcopedic textbook of contemporary constructions of psychopathology—and a detailed compendium of pornography. Within three years, they had obtained approval for its publication from Maxmillian I, emperor of the Holy Roman Empire, and from the faculty of theology of the University of Cologne. To paraphrase Alexander and Selesnick: The Witches' Hammer was thus supported by the imprimatur of the Vicar of Christ, that of the most powerful ruler of Europe, and that of the most important university in Christendom.[12]

Two themes predominate in the Witches' Hammer: a fierce misogyny and so paranoid a fear of behavior that is embarassing or irritating as to require an equation between such behavior and willful consortion with demons. Thus, any citizen whose symptoms would classify him or her today as mentally ill is categorically identified in the Witches' Hammer as a willful consort of Satan (i.e., as a witch), along with dissenters, schismatics, and heretics. And it is set forth in absolute terms that ''all witchcraft comes from carnal lust, which is in woman insatiable; wherefore, for the sake of fulfilling their lusts, they consort even with devils.''[13] Further, the operational definitions to be used to determine if one indeed consorts with demons are both simple and pointed and, in the main, fall within a psychiatric and psychological nosology: ''If he becomes dumb, deaf, insane, blind, which are the signs contained in the Holy Scriptures. . . If he feels stupid in the mind and takes pleasure in uttering stupidities and idiocies. . . If he has a disease and the disease is such that physicians cannot discover or diagnose it.''[14]

Quick dissolve. As we move to the next frame, we hear the voice of Martin Luther, raised *in support of* the Witches' Hammer.[15]

Next frame: we see before us the members of a Board of Inquisition someplace in Europe in the sixteenth century. Not only are there clerics but also civil judges and professors—specialists in the ''medicolegal science'' of witch-hunting, a science supported by such major figures in the history of medicine as Paracelsus and Ambrose Pare. Each inquisitor has been supplied with a copy of the Witches' Hammer printed in miniature so that ''Inquisitors might carry it in their pockets and read it under the table.''[16]

The accused enters. In Rosen's account, she is usually an old woman; her pubic hair has been shaved, so that the devil will not be able to hide here, in his favorite hiding place. She is asked to admit her guilt, renounce Satan, embrace Christ. Perhaps she does—sometimes, thanks to a ventriloquist employed by the Board of Inquisitors. If she declines, she is tortured. Still she refuses; she is exorcised. Yet she refuses; she is burned.[17] Under such circumstances, it should not surprise us that many of the accused were suddenly cured of diseases that were ''such that the physicians could not diagnose it.'' But these spontaneous remissions merely confirmed rather than contradicted the fixed constructions of inquisitors and faithful alike.

Of what monstrous crimes did the alleged witches stand accused?

According to Rosen, one confesses that she had enjoyed intercourse with Satan, who came to her in the form of her brother-in-law; another, that she had cast a spell upon her aging husband so as to cause him the loss of his virility. In Spanos' catalog, the accused "was typically an old, very poor, unmarried female . . . foulmouthed and unpleasant," but included "the socially disreputable: fornicators, blashphemers, thieves" and "priests . . . accused of witchcraft by demonically possessed nuns."[18]

Rapid dissolve. Let there now appear a stark legend: *There were hundreds of thousands of trials for witchcraft conducted over a period of 250 years after publication of the Witches' Hammer; tens of thousands of women, children, and men were executed as witches.* This legend is followed by the words of Friederich Spee, a German Jesuit serving as confessor to witches, written in 1631:

> Why do you search so diligently for sorcerers? I will show you at once where they are. Take the Capuchins, the Jesuits, all the religious orders, and torture them—they will confess. Should a few still be obstinate, exorcise them, shave them, keep on torturing—they will confess. If you want more, take the canons, the doctors, the bishops of the Church—they will confess. If you want still more, I will torture you and then you will torture me. I will confess and you will confess and so shall we all be sorcerers together.[19]

Spee's heroic (if anonymous) declaration is made during what Kirsch[20] regards as the very height of the witchcraft mania in Germany and for that reason alone looms as an act of rare courage. But it also reflects a growing sentiment in many parts of Christendom, poised beyond the threshold of Reformation but also no longer quite so threatened by a "new science" incompatible with the security and certainty of Revelation—indeed, a society, in Erikson's terms, beginning to relocate its boundaries so as to accommodate the spirit of challenge embodied not only in the theology of Erasmus, Melancthon, and Luther, but also in the physics of Galileo, Copernicus, and Kepler. That sentiment argued, if not yet entirely for abandoning a belief in demons, then at least for permitting a belief in culpable consortion with demons through witchcraft to subside in the direction of the more benign and more tolerant view of demoniac possession that had characterized a thousand years of Christianity before the Witches' Hammer and which seemed better attuned to the rhythm of a society whose boundaries, like it or not, were becoming more fluid.

Yet it is arguable that it required the witnessing of nearly three centuries of bureaucratically organized witch-hunting to activate older and more humane ways of construing psychopathological conditions, which, as Kirsch has it, saw demoniac possession as involuntary and supportiveness and group prayer as the most appropriate responses or, as Foucault has it, saw madness as a matter of divine sport.

Finally, there appeared in England a Sir Reginald Scot, formidable nemesis to the witch-hunters who earned the enmity of no less formidable a personality than King James I himself, and in Germany the physician Johann Weyer, who challenged the witchcraft mania on empirical medical grounds.[21] And in 1736 the British Parliament outlawed witch-hunting, for the second time, since the first such anti-witch-hunting law to be adopted by Parliament was quickly abandoned as unenforceable.[22] That second Parliamentary action brought substantial chagrin, one might note, to John Wesley, who wrote, "Giving up witchcraft is in effect giving up the Bible."[23]

At least officially, as Aldous Huxley put it, "The long orgy was at an end. If there had been no exorcists, it would never have begun."[24]

An Act of Parliament notwithstanding, the last witch to be burned in sovereign Britain was executed in Scotland in 1772; in the New World, the last official trial for sorcery took place in Mexico in 1874.[25] By that date, in Leipzig, Wilhelm Wundt had undertaken the series of experiments that were to lead, half a decade later, to the formal birth of modern scientific psychology; and, in Vienna, Sigmund Freud had embarked on his first year of medical studies.

Between 1550 B.C., when psychopathology had first been attributed to extranatural forces in a medical text, the superstitions of the cave art of earlier eras notwithstanding, and the last witch trial in the Western world, there had elapsed nearly 3,500 years of recorded human history—and there's been a little more than a hundred since.

Notes

1. Alexander and Selesnick, *The History of Psychiatry*, pp. 65-66. Psychiatrists Gregory Zilboorg and George W. Henry (*A History of Medical Psychology* [New York: Norton, 1941], p. 139) agree: "The idea that physical illnesses were natural and that mental illnesses were mostly supernatural became crystallized. People felt the need to differentiate. . . . The terms 'devil sickness' and 'witch disease' gained more and more frequent use."
2. Henry E. Sigerist, *Civilization and Disease* (Ithaca: Cornell University Press, 1945), p. 83.
3. George Rosen, *Madness in Society* (Chicago: University of Chicago Press, 1968), p. 8.
4. Erikson, *Wayward Puritans*, pp. 153-54. In a more recent analysis, Nicholas P. Spanos ("Witchcraft in Histories of Psychiatry: A Critical Analysis and an Alternative Conceptualization," *Psychological Bulletin*, 85 [1978], 417-39) opines similarly that the witchcraft mania had "little to do with a hypothetical upsurge in mental illness," but issued rather from "largely sociopolitical and economic factors."
5. Aldous Huxley, *The Devils of Loudon* (New York: Harper & Brothers, 1953), p. 14.
6. Alexander and Selesnick, *The History of Psychiatry*, p. 67.
7. Jacques Maritain, *Three Reformers: Luther–Descartes–Rousseau* (London: Sheed & Ward, 1941), pp. 183-84.
8. Bromberg, *The Mind of Man*, p. 31. Spanos, "Witchcraft in Histories of Psychiatry," traces the misogyny both to Christian tradition and to an increase in unmarried women in the late fifteenth century in a society in which "there were few acceptable roles for women outside of wife and mother. Women who did not somehow fall under the purview of a male dominated family were legally and economically helpless." Thus: "When to all of this is added a traditional misogyny, it is not surprising that it was poor, old, unmarried women, those members of society occupying among the most marginal and ambiguous social positions, who tended to be the subjects of unpopular stereotypes."
9. Rosen, *Madness in Society*, p. 11.
10. Hans Kuhner, *The Encylopedia of the Papacy* (New York: Philosophical Library, 1958), pp. 132-34.
11. The text of the Papal Bull *Summis desiderantes affectibus* is reproduced in Montague Summers, ed., *The Malleus Maleficaricum of Heinrich Kramer and James Sprenger* (London: John Rodker, 1928, 1948; New York: Dover, 1971), pp. xliii-xlv. The history of the decision to establish the process of Papal Inquisition as a uniform and centrally controlled means of combatting heresy during the twelfth century, as distinct from the decentralized, episcopally-controlled methods relied upon earlier, is

reviewed by the Augustinian Albert Clement Shannon, *The Popes and Heresy in the Thirteenth Century* (Villanova, Pa.: Augustinian Press, 1949), pp. 48-66. Jacob Burckhardt, in his classic *The Civilization of the Renaissance in Italy* (New York: Harper, 1958), pp. 501-9, examines the antecedents to the Papal assault on witchcraft, observing that Sixtus IV a decade earlier had proceeded against the Carmelites of Bologna who had asserted from their pulpits the absence of spiritual harm in seeking information from demons so long as no assistance in action was sought from that source—and perhaps offering as well to serve, for a fee, as intermediaries between Lucifer's knowledgable minions and those of the faithful who had little experience in necromancy. In a more recent account, Justo L. Gonzalez, *A History of Christian Thought from Augustine to the Eve of the Reformation* (Nashville: Abingdon Press, 1971), p. 225, gives a more sympathetic reading of Papal motives in the establishment of the Inquisition, regularized by precise rules of procedure: "The pope's purpose was to stop the abuses that often took place in the trial of heretics, where civil authorities used accusations of heresy for political or economic ends."

12. Alexander and Selesnick, *The History of Psychiatry*, p. 67. The letter of approbation from the faculty of Cologne is reproduced by Summers, *Malleus Maleficaricum*, pp. 275-78.

13. Summers, *Malleus Maleficaricum*, p. 47. The text continues: "There are three things that are never satisfied, yea, a fourth thing which says not, it is enough; that is, the mouth of the womb." A contemporary observer might conclude to a considerable obsession on the part of Kramer and Sprenger.

14. See Alexander and Selesnick, *The History of Psychiatry*, p. 68. The tests are detailed by Kramer and Sprenger in Question XVI, Part I, titled "The Foregoing Truths Are Set Out in Particular, by a Comparison of the Works of Witches with Other Baleful Superstitions" (Summers, *Malleus Maleficaricum*, pp. 80-88).

15. Maritain, *Three Reformers*, pp. 183-86, outlines Luther's deeply-rooted misogyny. The reformer's "base contempt for womanhood" more than a profound respect for Satan might account for his subscription to the underlying theses of Kramer and Sprenger.

16. Cited by Bromberg, *The Mind of Man*, p. 52.

17. Rosen, *Madness in Society*, p. 14.

18. Spanos, "Witchcraft in Histories of Psychiatry," opines that "Witchcraft accusations may have functioned as a means of defining the limits of acceptable behavior within a community" and "were typically supported and instigated by the accused's political and personal enemies."

19. Cited by Bromberg, *From Shaman to Psychotherapist*, p. 61. Substantial portions of the text of Spee's *Cautio Criminalis*, published anonymously, are reproduced in George L. Burr, *Translations and Reprints from the Original Sources of European History* (Philadelphia: University of Pennsylvania Press, 1897). Burr reports that authorship was not attributed until long after the Jesuit's death.

20. Irving Kirsch, "Demonology and the Rise of Science: An Example of the Misperception of Historical Data," *Journal of the History of the Behavioral Sciences* 14 (1978), 149-57.

21. Gregory Zilborg (*The Medical Man and the Witch During the Renaissance* [Baltimore: Johns-Hopkins University Press, 1935], pp. 109-207) regards Weyer as "the father of modern psychiatry." In his view: "Weyer's accomplishment was twofold: first, he introduced the scientific, descriptive, observational method to clinical psychopathology; and, second, he reclaimed the whole field of psychopathology for medicine." Szasz, in *The Manufacture of Madness*, especially pp. 71-72, 111-12, inclines to a less exalted evaluation.

22. Kirsch, "Demonology and the Rise of Science," p. 155; Bromberg, *From Shaman to Psychotherapist*, p. 63.

23. Cited by Bromberg, *From Shaman to Psychotherapist*, p. 62.

24. Huxley, *The Devils of Loudon*, p. 258.

25. Rosen, *Madness in Society*, p. 14. Likely the best-known of the many witchcraft trials in North America were those at Salem in 1692, subject of a commercially successful play (Arthur Miller's *The Crucible*) and innumerable scholarly studies by historians and behavioral scientists, some 15 of which have been collected by Marc Mappen in *Witches and Historians: Interpretations of Salem* (Huntington, NY: Robert E. Krieger, 1980). As Mappen says in his introduction, "By any measure, it was a relatively minor episode of the American Colonial era," yet "as much has been written about Salem as about the landing of the Mayflower or the signing of the Declaration of Independence."

6
Of Victorian Gentlemen and Closet Alcoholics

For our next vignette, we turn to *The Children of the Night*, a compila-
tion of Edward Arlington Robinson's verse composed between 1890
and 1905. Here we find the portrait of Richard Cory, "a gentleman
from sole to crown, clean-favored, imperially slim, richer than a
king . . ."

> *And admirably schooled in every grace;*
> *In fine, we thought that he was everything*
> *To make us wish that we were in his place.*
> *So on we worked, and waited for the light;*
> *And went without the meat and cursed the bread;*
> *And Richard Cory, one calm summer night,*
> *Went home and put a bullet through his head.*[1]

And it is apparent at once that poet Robinson, who knew not only
the irrationality of suicidally-depressed Richard's end but also that we
must continue both to do without the meat and to curse the bread, most
assuredly understood the social utility of psychopathological dis-ease.

The succeeding vignette comes from the curiosities of yesterday's
news. The time is 1978. We are in a small town in Georgia in the good
old U.S. of A. The scene is a gasoline filling station. We dolly in for a
close-up of a rather chubby gent in early middle age, dressed in jeans
and a denim shirt, somewhat greasy and unkempt; he is seated on a
chair tilted backwards at a rakish if precarious angle. When we're close

enough to see the stubble of beard on his face, he begins to speak, albeit rather incoherently—never mind that there is off-camera a fast-buck journalist who will soon condense these eminently forgettable utterances into a book entitled *The Wit and Widsom of Billy Carter*. The figure on camera regales us with his turgid, arcane views on politics, government, politicians, Jews, beer, and life in general. A few moments is enough to convince us that we have come face-to-face with a garden-variety redneck. This down-home lout is initially only mildly embarrassing to his older brother, who holds high elective office and lives in a big house up North. When he earns the universal antagonism of the press and then becomes a paid lobbyist for a foreign government, however, he becomes an active political liability.

Dissolve to a Spring afternoon a year later. The First Brother is holding a press conference outside the U.S. Naval Hospital in San Diego. He is thinner, grown a moustache, seems less aggressive, more polished—almost a likeable chap. He is explaining that only recently had he recognized that he had become an alcoholic, that he has now "taken the cure," that he now regards himself as a "recovering" alcoholic. The press is enamored of this "new" First Brother. His past indiscretions are explained and/or forgiven on the basis of a palpable psychiatric pathology; he is no longer held responsible for his embarrassing, irritating, dis-accommodating behavior during the days of his "closet" alcoholism, unrecognized by himself or by us—even when it becomes known that the military dictator of Libya holds the First Brother's promissory note for $220,000.

It takes no mean spirit to wonder whether contemporary psychiatry has been used most cynically for political ends.

Note

1. Edward Arlington Robinson, "Richard Cory," *The Children of the Night* (New York: Charles Scribner's Sons, 1905).

7

Contemporary Care for the Mentally Ill

A self-congratulatory slide show represents the conceit for this vignette. The first slide can be entitled "The Impact of the Federal Community Mental Health Act on Mental Health Care in the United States." On the first line, we read: After an eight-year period of study, the federal Congress adopted the Community Mental Health Act of 1963 to provide outpatient services to the mentally ill who might otherwise be remanded to psychiatric hospitals. A key element in this decision was the well-founded observation of progressive deterioration in hospitalized mental patients, so that the legislation essentially sought to prevent further incidence of progressive deterioration by making mental health care available to the psychopathologically disordered and/or dis-eased in the communities where they live. (Flourish of trumpets.)

The second line: In 1950, thirteen years before the Community Mental Health Act was adopted, for each 100,000 of the U.S. population, there were 406 men, women, and children hospitalized in mental institutions.

Third line: By 1970, before the community mental health program became as fat and sassy as it is today, but the last year for which accurate data are available even today, there were only 214 men, women, and children hospitalized in mental institutions for each 100,000 of the United States population—slightly over half as many as in 1950.

Fourth line: By 1970, community mental health centers treated twice as many patients as did mental hospitals.[1]

Fifth line: We call *this* progress. Flourish; drum roll; fanfare.

Dissolve to the next slide. But, surprisingly, that one looks like it's part of a different series, with its handwritten scratches instead of fine, clear, crisp, bureaucratic block printing. Anyway, it says: According to a report published by a group of University of Maryland researchers in 1977, 76 percent of all patient contact hours in all Federally funded Community Mental Health Centers in the United States were delivered by paraprofessionals—that is, by persons below the bachelor's degree in formal educational preparation. Only 24 percent of all patient contact service hours were delivered by psychiatrists, psychologists, social workers, registered nurses, and non-psychiatrist physicians put together.[2]

And it also says: Are you sure you want to call *that* progress?

The next slide: the Federal Judiciary Affirms the Right to Treatment for Patients in Public Mental Hospitals.

It reads: In 1971, Wyatt, a patient at Bryce Mental Hospital in Alabama, brought suit against the state for failure to provide mental health treatment, alleging that instead he was being confined against his will and was being accorded only custodial care. In a series of landmark decisions through 1975, the federal courts affirmed the right of mental patients in public mental hospitals to treatment, along the way establishing standards to govern the ratio between patients and professional treatment staff as well as other aspects of hospital operation.[3] And the editorial note: *These decisions are yet other benchmarks on the path of man's progress in the treatment of the psychopathologically disordered and dis-eased. Flourish; fanfare.*

One more line, again lacking crisp block printing. It seems to say: *Before* the Wyatt decision, Alabama's state budget for mental hospitals was $36 million and the patient population was 10,000. *After* the Wyatt decision, the budget had increased 230 percent to $83 million, but the patient population had been reduced 58 percent to 4200.[4] Are you sure you want to call *that* progress?

Only one more slide. Its title: The Relationship between Social Class and Mental Illness. On it, we read: For four decades, the relationship between social class and mental illness has been studied carefully by a wide array of competent social scientists with remarkably consistent findings:[5]

That such severely disabling mental illness as schizophrenia is much more likely, in some studies twice as likely, to be found among members of the lower social classes than among members of the middle or upper classes; that the rate of admission to public mental hospitals is much higher, in some studies nearly twice as high, among members of the lower classes; that members of the middle and upper classes are much more frequently treated by private mental health practitioners in outpatient settings utilizing therapeutic techniques usually thought to be associated with more positive therapeutic outcomes; that lower class patients are much more frequently given only medication without other treatment or confined to public mental hospitals largely for custodial care, again without treatment.[6]

Clearly a message is intended here, poorly disguised, barely hidden amongst all those data:

- Because they suffer the more severe of the discernible psychological disorders, the poor are in greater need of mental health care, such as that we in our naivete believe should be provided in well-operated mental hospitals funded from the public treasury.
- As a humanely caring society, we have undertaken a massive effort to decrease the rate of hospitalization in mental institutions.
- As a humanely caring society, we have substituted a network of in vivo community mental health centers for the in vitro environments of mental hospitals.

Thus, it seems to follow, the psychopathologically disordered and dis-eased poor are more likely than anyone else to need intensive mental health treatment. That accounts for why the poor used to be admitted to public mental hospitals at such a great rate. But we have reduced the relative populations of the mental hospitals in favor of outpatient treatment in community mental health centers. That makes it as it should be, because now the psychopathologically disordered and dis-eased poor are not so readily admitted to public mental hospitals, where they probably would not have gotten much more than medication and custodial care anyway; instead, they are treated in community mental health centers—*by paraprofessionals.*

So this slide show, it seems, asserts that we've been engaged in a giant shell game, a plot constructed by a humanely caring society to cool the mark, to ensure that those members of the society who are both psychopathologically and economically disordered—who, the research says, most need, but are least able to afford, mental health care—are given only services substandard by customary professional yardsticks, whether in public mental hospitals or in the community.

But surely people who are confined for long terms to mental hospitals really do deteriorate; surely the wide-scale introduction of mental health services in the communities has been in the direction of genuine progress; just as surely, by emptying the mental hospitals in favor of community-based care of whatever level of quality, we have also substantially increased the community's level of tolerance for the patently psychologically disordered and/or dis-eased—or is it just that we have made them more visible?

Now that is downright confusing. We might be better off to reject this vignette, with its mawkish effort to convince us that we are the dupes of some covert social policy created by a conspiracy of folks off-camera whose presence is felt but never observed, that most of the rest of us are not even puppets but only adjectives or adverbs in a pervasive script whose sole purpose is to ensure that the deviant remain deviant.

Notes

1. Morton Kramer reports the data reviewed here in *Psychiatric Services and the Changing Institutional Scene, 1950-85* (Rockville, Md.: National Institute of Mental Health, 1977), pp. 19-26, . The development of community mental health centers has been reviewed in a number of works, including Sheldon Korchin's *Modern Clinical Psychology* (New York: Basic Books, 1976).
2. These data are reported by Dan Tweed, Mildred Konan, and James W. Longest, *Distribution of Mental Health Manpower in the United States* (College Park, Md.: Division of Agriculture and Life Sciences, University of Maryland, 1977), pp. 4, 52-61.

3. Mr. Justice Johnson's opinions and rulings in the landmark cases—*Wyatt v. Stickney* (1972), *Wyatt v. Aderhold* (1974), and *Wyatt v. Hardin* (1975)--are reproduced in full by Stuart Golann and William J. Fremouw, eds., *The Right to Treatment for Mental Patients* (New York: Irvington, 1976), pp. 129-85. Golann discusses appellate decisions in these cases in his Epilog, pp. 123-25.

4. See the remarkable eyewitness account by the initial defendant-of-record, Stonewall B. Stickney, in *"Wyatt v. Stickney:* Background and Postscript," in Golann and Fremouw, *The Right to Treatment for Mental Patients,* pp. 29-46. Dr. Stickney was relieved of his post as Alabama's Commissioner of Mental Hygiene by Governor George Wallace for his purported collusion with plaintiffs in framing their cases.

5. The relevant citations follow in chronological order: Robert E.L. Faris and H. Warren Dunham, *Mental Disorders in Urban Areas* (Chicago: University of Chicago Press, 1939); August de B. Hollingshead and Frederick C. Redlich, *Social Class and Mental Illness* (New York: Wiley, 1958); Jerome K. Myers and Bertram H. Roberts, *Family and Class Dynamics in Mental Illness* (New York: Wiley, 1959); Srole et al., *Mental Health in the Metropolis* (1962); Jerome K. Myers and Lee L. Bean, *A Decade Later* (New York: Wiley, 1968); Bruce P. Dohrenwend and Barbara Snell Dohrenwend, *Social Status and Psychological Disorder* (New York: Wiley, 1969).

6. John A. Clausen, "Mental Disorders," in Merton and Nisbet, eds., *Contemporary Social Problems* (New York: Harcourt, Brace, Jovanovich, 1971), pp. 79-87; Herbert Goldhamer and Andrew W. Marshall, *Psychosis and Civilization* (Glencoe, Ill.: Free Press, 1949); Marvin K. Opler, *Culture and Social Psychiatry* (New York: Atherton, 1967).

8
Outpatient Psychotherapy for the Poor

After those disappointing slides, we turn to a short documentary film for our next vignette.

Its title, promising to tell all in typical Hollywood fashion, might be: "How Psychotherapy for the Poor Really Helps—You and Me," and its subtitle, borrowed from an address by Mr. Justice David Bazelon,[1] might be "Are professional psychotherapists doing good for their clients—or well for themselves?"

The film begins with a patient, a black woman who lives in an inner city (we could make it New Brunswick, New Jersey, for that matter). Because she is an unmarried "welfare mother," she is entitled to Medicaid health care benefits from the Federal and state governments. She is preparing to visit her fully professional, doctoral-level, even Board-certified psychotherapist at a private clinic; she can do so, avoiding the putatively substandard care she's likely to get in a community mental health center, because she holds title to those Medicaid benefits. She boards a taxi and arrives at the office, which, as the office of private practitioners often are, is located in a medical center in a nice, predominantly white, suburban community; let us say, for purposes of the example, that it is East Brunswick.

She's a certified schizophrenic, with a ten year history of intermittent hospitalization for that pernicious dis-ease, one symptom of which is a cleavage between cognitive and conative functioning; even so, many of the life problems she discusses with her therapist issue from the fact that, even with the welfare dole, food stamps, and Medicaid, she and her four children live well below the poverty level, so that she can begin to satisfy few of the aspirations the media have taught her she must have for herself and her children to qualify as first-class members of the society. She has her session with her therapist (I might even be he), then leaves for home via taxi.

The fun begins when we start to calculate the costs for this session. New Jersey pays $37 per therapeutic hour for outpatient therapy done by a state-licensed, board-certified psychiatrist or psychologist. Federal and state regulations, however, also permit payment for reasonable transportation costs to and from the therapy session—in this case, $12 each way, $24 round trip. So, in New Jersey, the tab for this session runs to $61. Other states are not so niggardly; their rates of payment are higher, and some pick up the tab for therapy sessions in community mental health centers as well as in private clinics—even when those sessions are conducted by paraprofessionals. The cost of transportation applies in any case, and the mode of transportation is inevitably the taxi; how else can one get from the inner city to those suburban medical centers?

Those figures are instructive: $61 per session, one session per week, four weeks per month, 12 months per year. That works out to $244 a month (*or the equivalent of 60 percent of this patient's total monthly income for herself and her four children from the welfare dole and food stamps put together*) and $2,928 a year—of which $1,152 goes to the cab company.
    We are now in a position to trace how the funds which come *from* the public treasury are plowed *back into* the general economy by the psychotherapist, his receptionist, the people who rent him his office space, supply the heat, print his business cards, repair his tape recorder and personal computer—*and also* by the cab driver, the people who run the gas station where he trades, the folks who sell him his snow tires, the PBA that sells him tickets to the Policemen's Ball, not to mention the bookkeepers, key-punch operators, computer programmers, program auditors, and other civil servants at state and Federal levels required to push the paper that makes it all happen.
    Now *that's* how psychotherapy for the poor really works—for *me* and *you*.

Is it in the least a tenable hypothesis that we could aid the general economy equally well were we to say to this patient, here's an extra $244 each month, take the kids out, buy them some fancy clothes, go to the beach, head for the track, take the bundle and blow it on the crap tables in Atlantic City? Might not that extra income give this patient a greater sense of membership in a competitive society where one's worth as a person is measured by one's buying power? And, in turn, might not all of that just have some beneficial effect on her psychopathological dis-ease, a major symptom of which is a cleavage between cognitive and conative functioning?

But the alternative here described seems like some Che-inspired prescription for the redistribution of wealth. And that, most emphatically, is not the purpose of the welfare system, nor what we had in mind at all when, as members of a humanely caring society, we decided to provide, through Medicaid, an alternate to sub-standard mental hospitals and community mental health centers for the psychopathologically disordered and dis-eased poor.

Many in our humanely caring society believe that the purpose of the welfare system is to help the poor; others, diametrically, that we taxpayers are entirely too generous with the size of the dole. Both groups exhibit gross naivete. The purpose for welfare seems far more universal and sophisticated—to provide consumers for the products of our factories and customers for our stores. Its ultimate benefactees are the stockholders of the major corporations; but that is as it should be, since they are the folks who kick in the largest share to the public treasury to support the system anyway—unless of course their accountants are competent enough to discover an integrated system of tax shelters.

The last frame slips into rapid motion. We see our example repeated hundreds, thousands of times, until the images blur and all the motion seems circular. There's a voice-over narration by Ivan Illich:

> The progressive fragmentation of needs into ever smaller and unconnected parts makes the client dependent on professional judgment for the blending of his needs into a meaningful whole. To be plugged into a professional system as a life-long client is no longer a stigma. . . . *We now live in a society organized for deviant majorities and their keepers.* To be an active client provides you with a well-defined place within the realm of consumers for the sake of whom our society functions.[2]

Or, in the more sterile tones of formal social science, Scheff has it that psychiatric "labelling" of the sort involved in a formal diagnosis itself both proves comforting to the person whose behavior is so described and establishes a distinct role for him or her to play, so that the very act of labelling yields cues for the continuation of behavior that is embarrassing, irritating, or otherwise dis-accommodating: "Labelling thus creates a pattern of 'symptomatic' behavior in conformity with the stereotyped expectations of others. To the extent that the deviant's role becomes a part of the deviant's self-conception, his ability to control his own behavior may actually become impaired."[3]

So, it appears, Illich in dramatic (if not inflammatory) terms and Scheff in the sterile sounds of science conclude that the more we provide help to those we have identified as disordered, or who identify themselves as dis-eased, the more likely the recipients of that help are to behave in ways that are irritating, embarrassing, dis-accommodating; or, more simply, is it that the more we help those who are disordered and dis-eased, the more disordered and dis-eased those whom we help become?

Notes

1. David L. Bazelon, "Psychologists in Corrections: Are They Doing Good for the Offender or Well for Themselves?" in Stanley Brodsky, ed., *Psychologists in the Criminal Justice System* (Urbana, Ill.: University of Illinois Press, 1973), pp. 149-54.
2. Ivan Illich, *Toward a History of Needs* (New York: Pantheon, 1978), pp. 32-33. Illich's view is that, in a society organized for deviant majorities and their keepers, clienthood confers status and personhood. Rather in contrast, Sarbin and Mancuso, *Schizophrenia: Medical Diagnosis or Moral Verdict*, pp. 217-18, hold that the conferring of clienthood by means especially of diagnostic labels in essence "designates a degraded social identity. . . . The pejorative label . . . is assigned by mental health workers. The label serves the same function as visible stigmata of degradation."
3. Thomas J. Scheff, "The Societal Reaction to Deviance: Ascriptive Elements in the Psychiatric Screening of Mental Patients in a Midwestern State Hospital," *Social Problems* 11 (1964), 401-13. See also Scheff's *Being Mentally Ill: A Sociological Theory* (Chicago: Aldine, 1966); David Mechanic, *Mental Health and Social Policy* (Englewood Cliffs, N.J.: Prentice-Hall, 1980), pp. 94-106.

9

Virtue Freely Chosen

In this cavalcade of vignettes, we turn to *A Clockwork Orange*, a fictional rendition by Antony Burgess of the psychological history of Alex, a delinquent 15-year-old in London at some unspecified future date. He is much given to Beethoven's Ninth Symphony, which conjures within him images of violence to be perpetrated upon others senselessly, aimlessly, mercilessly, and repeatedly—because it provides its own reward. In Alex's words:

> All right, I do bad, what with crasting and tolchoks and carves with the britva and the old in-out, in-out [that translates to robbery, beating, knifing, and rape] and if I get loveted [caught], well, too bad for me . . . so if I get loveted and it's three months in this mesto [reformatory] and another six in that and then, in spite of the great tenderness of my summers, brothers, it's the great unearthly zoo itself [prison], well I say "Fair, but a pity" . . . [because] I am serious with you, brothers, over this—what I do I do because I *like* to do.[1]

In the space of approximately three days, Alex and his three companions beat an old man senseless; invade a suburban cottage, beat the husband mercilessly, and multiply rape the wife; and rape two eleven-year-old girls. During the commission of a burglary, Alex murders an old woman. He is caught and imprisoned. During the course of his imprisonment, he deliberately and cynically, in hopes of parole, ingratiates the prison chaplain. The prison is, as usual worldwide, overcrowded. After two years, another prisoner, a homosexual, is added to the already crowded cell occuppied by Alex and several others; Alex murders him.

It seems to require little expertise psychiatrically or judicially to pronounce Alex incorrigible. But, instead of prosecution for yet another murder, Alex is given the *choice* of undergoing a new rehabilitative treatment called "Ludovici's technique"—and of being released in two weeks. Alex gives his *consent* with alacrity.

Ludovici's technique consists essentially of a variant of behavioral counter-conditioning (or, more technically, aversive conditioning), coupled with the use of psychoactive medication—a close analogue to methods that in actuality are well-developed and currently available in the clinical treatment of criminals and noncriminals alike. At the end of the treatment, Alex becomes massively dis-eased both physically and psychologically at the merest thought of the violence that once exhilarated him.

Happy ending? Not quite yet. Alex is incapable of doing evil. The result much troubles the prison chaplain: "What does God want? Does God want goodness or the *choice* of goodness? Is the man who chooses the bad perhaps in some way better than the man who has the good imposed upon him?"

The rehabilitated Alex is indeed released in two weeks, on the eve of a general election called by the prime minister. In short order, he is disowned by his parents, beaten by a cohort of old men he had attacked years ago, beaten by the police—and befriended by the man whose cottage he had invaded and whose wife he had raped; the latter is now deceased, perhaps by her own hand.

Alex's new friend, the surviving husband, is an activist of the doctrinnaire Old Left, intensely committed to libertarianism as a political and economic philosophy. Campaigning for a change in government, he sees in Alex, the story of whose rehabilitation has now become front-page, major political capital. He first elicits from Alex the story of his dehumanization at the hands of the behaviorists who have rendered him incapable of evil, to be published in the opposition press; he then arranges a set of stimulus conditions such that Alex has no option but to attempt suicide. Not to be outdone, the Government arranges for Alex to be counter-conditioned once again—to be returned to the state of his violent psychopathy before undergoing Ludovici's treatment. That counter-counter-conditioning is indeed successful; Alex emerges once again as a violent psychopath; the press is pleased; the Government is reelected.

In the story of Alex, novelist Burgess gives us two options: A person incapable of genuine choice but bent upon psychopathic violence *or* a person incapable of genuine choice but also incapable of violence. Burgess has society prefer the former.

Alex's story is fictional. Sometimes, but only sometimes, art imitates life. Consider this account, reported by Hans Eysenck, of the real-life treatment of an adult patient whose crimes do not begin to rival Alex's. The "patient," a man of 33, suffers from fetishism—the attachment of sexual significance to neutral objects, in this case handbags and baby carriages—expressed behaviorally in a rather bizarre way. Since the age of 10, he has on numerous occasions slashed baby carriages or set them on fire, perhaps as often as two or three times per week; he has damaged handbags even more frequently. Though he has undergone psychoanalytic treatment and has thereby relived several childhood experiences which explain the symbolic significance of the objects of his attacks—both carriages and purses are for him, symbolically, "enclosed female places"—there has been no improvement in his embarrassing, irritating behavior. After his twelfth arrest, he is treated as an inpatient in a London psychiatric hospital through an aversion therapy regimen utilizing behavioral counter-conditioning supported by injections of Apomorphine, a powerful emetic "which produces sickness and vomiting after a short period of time." Eysenck's account of the treatment and its course:

> It was explained to the patient that the aim of treatment was to alter his attitude to handbags and perambulators by teaching him to associate them with an unpleasant sensation instead of a pleasurable, erotic sensation. Although he was frankly skeptical about the treatment, he said he was willing to try anything.[2]

Whether the patient had any intimation of the particular direction the "learning experience" in store for him would take is not recorded; but let Eysenck continue:

> A collection of handbags, perambulators, and coloured illustrations was obtained and these were shown to the patient after he had received an

injection of Apomorphine and just before nausea was produced. The treatment was given two-hourly day and night, no food was allowed, and amphetamine was used to keep him awake. At the end of the first week, treatment was temporarily suspended . . . Five days after the treatment had re-commenced, he said that the mere sight of the objects made him sick. On the evening of the ninth day, he rang his bell and was found to be sobbing uncontrollably. He kept repeating, ''Take them away,'' and appeared to be impervious to anything that was said to him. The sobbing continued unabated until the objects were removed and he was given a sedative.[2]

Alex's fictional rehabilitation was short-lived; society decreed that he should be returned to a state of violent psychopathy in order to demonstrate the commitment of Her Majesty's Government to the principles of libertarianism. What of Eysenck's real-life patient, whose antisocial behavior alongside Alex's is quite pale?

Nineteen months after he had first had aversion therapy . . . the patient reports that he no longer requires the old fantasies to enable him to have sexual intercourse. . . . The wife reports that she is no longer constantly worrying about the possibility of police action against him. Their sexual relations ''have greatly improved.'' The probation officer reports that the patient has made ''very noticeable progress'' . . . he has been promoted to a more responsible job and he has not been in trouble with the police.

In a somewhat macabre footnote, let it be observed that one paradoxical but common side effect of Apomorphine is euphoria. The possibilities for misadventure might stagger the imagination—until, of course, we realize that such powerful medication would never be administered in our public mental hospitals or prisons in the absence of that high level of intensive medical supervision we have learned to associate with those institutions.

Alex, central figure in a work of fiction, was not administered Ludovici's treatment until he had given his specific consent. In fact, unlike fiction, there is no record that the specific consent of Eysenck's patient was elicited, though we are told that he had grown desperate enough ''to try anything.''

Both that fiction and that fact were set on the other side of the Atlantic. In our humanely caring society, which has enlisted armies of people-helpers and everywhere exhibits libertarian principles, we have by decision of the federal courts insured that nothing like the sort of treatment accorded Alex or Eysenck's patient could easily be perpetrated in our name. Consider the order of Mr. Justice Frank M. Johnson, Jr., in the case of *Wyatt v. Hardin*, the landmark case of the half-century in respect of the rights of mental patients: "No patient shall be [involuntarily] subjected to any aversive conditioning or other systematic attempt to alter his behavior by means of noxious stimuli." The only condition under which Mr. Johnson's order permits aversive treatment is one in which:

> The patient has given his *express and informed consent in writing* to the administration of aversive conditioning. It shall be the responsibility of the treating psychiatrist to provide the patient with complete and accurate information concerning the nature and effects of aversive therapy, to assist the patient in comprehending the significance of such information, and to identify any barriers to such comprehension. The written consent signed by the patient shall include a statement of the nature of the treatment consented to; a description of its purpose, risks, and possible effects; and a notice to the patient that he has *the right to terminate his consent* at any time and for any reason.

Mr. Johnson also ordered the formation in each mental hospital of an "Extraordinary Treatment Committee," to be appointed by the court and not to include any member of the staff of the Department of Mental Health or anyone else involved in the proposed treatment, which has as its primary responsibility "to determine, after appropriate inquiry and interview with the patient, whether the patient's consent is in fact knowing, intelligent, and voluntary."[3]

Which is fact and which is fiction? Or the theater of the absurd?

Contemporary psychopharmocology, medicine, psychology, and penology collude to devise powerful, even frightening, means to extirpate the motives for, and the satisfactions attached to, those forms of behavior that we find so irritating as to label criminal. Perhaps in consequence of libertarian principles, perhaps only because we believe that God wants the *choice* of goodness more than goodness itself, other forces generated by other engines conspire to insure that these means will be applied only to those who are able to give, and to retract, "knowing, informed, and voluntary" consent *before* the treatment is applied—that is, to those who are, a priori, capable of "*choosing* the good."

One of the better-known of the current commentaries on America's prison system is the volume *Struggle for Justice*, a publication of the American Friends Service Committee, which contains a chapter devoted to our clinically-oriented penology called "The Crime of Treatment."[4] And there hangs an irony, for the penitentiary is itself the invention of the American Friends. The first such institution, established near Philadelphia in the late eighteenth century, is described as "a product of Quaker thinking and planning [that] bore the stamp of Quaker theology for the stated purpose [of giving] the inmate a chance to come to terms with his inner self"[5]—that is, to do penance. Before the invention of the penitentiary, a non-humanely caring society sent criminals to prisons to confine and to punish them; after that humanely caring invention, we send criminals to places where, by doing penance, they might become rehabilitated.

Is it a tenable hypothesis that, had the Quakers of the 1770s not invented places for organized penance, the Quakers of the 1970s might have found less to denounce in contemporary correctional practices?

But it is not only inexorable but desirable that societal values change, as well they might; penance at one moment, punishment the next; sometimes with a concern for libertarian principles, other times not; and the only question ever open has been and remains who is to be victimized, by whom, and when.

With only a slight variation on the theme, we once again encounter the spectre of a script whose purpose is to ensure that the deviant remain deviant.

Notes

1. Anthony Burgess, *A Clockwork Orange* (New York: Norton, 1963), p. 43.
2. Hans J. Eysenck, *Crime and Personality* (London: Routledge & Kegan Paul, 1977), pp. 169-71.
3. Cited in Golann and Fremouw, *The Right to Treatment for Mental Patients*, pp. 179-85.
4. American Friends Service Committee, *Struggle for Justice* (New York: Hill & Wang, 1971).
5. Erikson, *Wayward Puritans*, pp. 200-204. For a reading of the elements in society which led to the development of prisons, see Michel Foucault, *Discipline and Punish: The Birth of the Prison* (New York: Pantheon, 1978).

10

The Parable of Sunrise House

Fie, fie! Enough of vignettes! Put the last dozen pages down to cynicism run amok, perhaps itself the product of some psychological disease that manifests itself in acerbic intellectualisms with the flavor of the lunatic left.

Cynicism cast aside, the facts are plain and their interpretation simple. We *are* a humanely caring society; we have recognized that psychological disorder and dis-ease abound; in response, we have conspired to make psychotherapeutic treatment the responsibility not only of card-carrying doctoral-level professionals in medicine, psychiatry, and psychology, but also of that army of other people-helpers, disorder-remediers, and dis-ease-alleviators to whom earlier references have been unsubtly derisive; we have required that the costs associated with that treatment be borne by the public dole through Medicaid and Medicare or by the fat-cat insurers legislatively licensed to write health insurance at rapidly escalating rates, with both decisions monuments to the social consciences of our federal and state legislators, perhaps appropriately informed by an occasional contact with lobbyists who represent the interests of the providers of such treatment; we have stimulated and/or encouraged the development of new techniques and forms of treatment to add to the arsenal from which both the professionals and the paraprofessionals who serve in those phalanxes arm themselves. Yet we have also taken judicial and/or legislative precautions to insure that neither the new army nor the new techniques violate those personal liberties we prize so highly. Inevitably, these new and some-times unorthodox techniques and the new dis-ease-alleviators have yielded new configurations for the delivery of disorder-remedying and dis-ease-alleviating services, new conceptualizations of the psycho-therapeutic process itself, and perhaps even new definitions of psychopathology and its obverse.

The parable of the rise and fall of Sunrise House can provide us an ob-ject lesson both in broad-gauged, contemporary psychological treat-ment aimed at the extirpation of behavior that is dangerous, irritating, disaccommodating *and* in the contextual issues relating to the new configuration of services, the new disorder-remedying and dis-ease-alleviating processes, and indeed in new views of psychopathology it-self.

The parable of Sunrise House, essentially factual but rendered here with fictional names to protect guilty and innocent alike, begins with the early criminal history of Dave Duncan. Dave is a native of Chicago's South Side; as he put it, he graduated from petty theft at the age of five to armed robbery by the time he was thirteen. As a post-graduate course, he apprenticed himself as a dealer in cocaine and hashish, along the way acquiring a $200 a day habit himself. By the time he was 20, he'd been in and out of reformatory and prison so often he'd lost count.

During his final period of residence in the slammer, Dave stumbled upon what was apparently quite a catholic prison library, one which had been built to develop skills other than those required by jailhouse lawyers in the preparation of their interminable appeals. So, in quite a new experience for him, he began to read widely: psychology at first, then philosophy and political theory. Among the works he sought were those of Freud and Jung, Carl Rogers and the phenomenologists, Glas-ser and the reality therapists, Wolpe and the behaviorists. But he also came upon *The Wretched of the Earth* by an Algerian psychiatrist named Frantz Fanon, and that led him to Marx, Nasser, Castro, Mao.

By the time he had digested, or perhaps half-digested, all those ideas in all those books, Dave found himself in the throes of an internal con-version. He vowed to foresake forever a lifestyle characterized by crime and drugs; further, he convinced himself that he now had avail-able within himself the inner resources to help others make and abide by the same decision. For he had come to understand that, in his sordid career as criminal, drug addict, drug pusher, he had been not an aggressor but a victim, that what he now (in rather a paroxysm of self-congratulation over this remarkable insight) saw as a capitalist society had decreed that he should be born into an ethnic ghetto, compelling him to learn to survive by the law of jungle and fang.

Armed with a new sense of purpose and the zeal not of the apostle but of the founding father himself, Dave came to New York City. Through one means and another, often putting to good use the occupational skills characteristic of the con man he had once been, Dave acquired a house and grounds on Staten Island and set about putting into practice his "therapeutic" plans for people-helping. Along with several other former addicts, he founded Sunrise House, a residential treatment program for narcotics addicts to be operated and staffed solely by ex-addicts like himself.

Sunrise proved rather selective with respect to whom it deigned to accept for "treatment," but its results were astounding even so. At a time when the model U.S. Public Health Service Hospital in Lexington, Kentucky, cited a "success" rate in the treatment of addicts such that no more than 8 percent remained drug-free two years after discharge and the massive program operated by the New York State Narcotics Addiction Control Commission cited a success rate of 22 percent against the same criterion, Sunrise claimed success in 75 percent of its cases. Pointedly and in contrast to the massive public dollars behind Lexington and the Narcotics Commission, Sunrise supported itself entirely through contributions and through the sale of handcrafted items produced in its cottage industries.

Federal and state agencies have a way of noticing successful private programs, especially when those programs seem to yield high degrees of success, and it happened that, just as Sunrise came to public attention on a local and regional basis, the Johnson administration, having waged its war on poverty, now mounted a crusade against mind-altering chemicals. So federal and state officials came to Sunrise with offers of public funding for program expansion and development. Reluctantly at first, Dave and his cohorts agreed to accept public monies "in partial support" of their sterling program and its expansion.

Much of the federal money went into financing a new venture for Sunrise—a program of prevention based on "outreach" into the community—beyond its residential treatment for those already addicted. Sunrise opened a series of store fronts in the ghettos of Manhattan and the South Bronx. The outreach program, in conformance with the categorial imperatives of federally-funded social programs, was code-named Operation Bridgehead, and at its center stood a program element acronymically called GUTS.

With federal dollars comes federal regulation, then federal inspection, and finally federal control. As one condition for the public dole, Sunrise's founders had instituted a formal governance structure replete with a board of directors composed of mental health and social service professionals and representatives of the power elite. After a decent interval came federal program auditors for a full-blown on-site inspection, bent on evaluating whether Sunrise's outreach program was on its way to achieving the objectives for which it had been funded—that is, the prevention of addiction among groups at high risk for such addiction.

It is reported that the federal inspectors were marvelously impressed with Sunrise's residential treatment facility on Staten Island but that they resisted several unsubtle attempts to persuade them to confine their site inspection to that locale which, after all, received little federal support. So on they pressed for the Operation Bridgehead sites, somewhat aggressively and with just a hint of self-righteousness, as befits federal inspectors.

At the typical Bridgehead store-front, the inspectors encountered a first floor comprised of counseling offices and small group rooms, along with the usual audio-visual equipment to show horror films of the effects of addiction and literature in two languages. But in the basement they found GUTS: libraries of revolutionary writings, instructions on how to construct pipe bombs, maps highlighting the city's power stations and subway and rail systems, and a pistol range with the likenesses of New York City policemen and U.S. Army infantrymen as targets. And they discovered that GUTS was an acronym for Guerrilla Urban Training Station.

With a speed not customary in a bureaucracy, it was decided that, in consequence of his personal role in what was tantamount to mismanagement of federal funds if not downright fraud, Dave had to go. In a display of uncharacteristic magnanimity, the funding agency determined to continue funding for Operation Bridgehead (a decision that provided a field day for the press), but only if GUTS were eliminated from the program. The mental health and social service professionals and other radical-chic representatives of the power elite who comprised the Sunrise House board of directors, in the fullness of their conviction that the proper role for Sunrise lay in preventing and treating addiction and most assuredly not in radicalizing the proletariat, solemnly and dully demanded Dave's immediate resignation.

To the amazement of all but his intimates, Dave decided to resign with barely a peep of protest, though the evidence seemed clear and overwhelming that Sunrise and Bridgehead had been wildly successful in the goals they pursued with respect to treatment and to prevention, with whatever else these programs had also accomplished beyond these clear and explicit goals bracketed to one side.

But Dave confessed that he was ready to abandon Sunrise in any case—as a failure, for, in his judgment, "Of the 75 percent of those we've treated 'successfully,' only 10 percent have committed to the revolutonary cause; the other 65 percent have gotten jobs, gotten married, bought cars, are living in the suburbs—they have become part of the bourgeoisie which oppresses."

Consider two points from the parable of Sunrise House. First, the funding agency never argued that Sunrise had not achieved the specific purposes for which a humanely caring society had funded it, first privately, then publicly. Instead, the funding agency objected that the public's money had been used for purposes which, however incidentally alleviating of psychological dis-ease or remedial of psychological disorder (in this instance, accompanied to be sure by physical pathology into the bargain), went quite beyond those specific purposes *with which it agreed*. There was, in that process, a value judgment of monumental proportions—viz., the judgment that it is socially more acceptable in a humanely caring society to remain addicted than to become politically radicalized as a by-product of emancipation from the physical and psychological bondage of addiction.

Second, contrast Dave Duncan's criterion for success with that of the funding agency. Dave wanted *more* than to cure an addict of his biochemical burden; he wanted to bring that addict to a state of radical political awareness so that he could share Dave's view of the politics, economics, and sociology of addiction, could see addiction as a mechanism both to pacify and to regulate segments of the population who might otherwise threaten the established order of things. According to that criterion, Sunrise had been successful in only 10 percent of its cases; in the 25 percent of the cases where there had been no change in the pattern of drug use, it had been unsuccessful; but in the 65 percent of the cases in which its patients had both forsaken drugs and become middle class in their orientation, the results of the treatment had been directly negative. For the funding agency, Sunrise had been successful only in that 65 percent of the cases that Dave saw not merely as failures but as having produced directly negative outcomes.

As an apostrophe, consider Ivan Illich's indictment of what he calls "the age of the disabling professions:"

> These new specialists, who are usually *servicers of the human needs their specialty has defined*, tend to wear the mask of love and to provide some form of care. . . . Merchants sell you the goods they stock. Guildsmen guarantee quality. Some craftspeople tailor their product to your measure or fancy. These professionals [in the human services], however, tell you what you need. They claim the power to prescribe. *They not only advertise what is good but ordain what is right*.[1]

As a postscript, we might report that, when we last heard from him, Dave Duncan signed himself as president of an organization head-quartered in San Francisco called Ideas West, Ltd., on stationery trumpeting that Ideas West is a management consulting firm specializing in employee motivation training.

Radicalizing the proletariat or becoming part of the bourgeoisie which oppresses?

Note

1. Ivan Illich, *Toward a History of Needs* (New York: Pantheon, 1978), pp. 23-24.

11

The Criterion Problem
in Professional Psychotherapy

So much for Sunrise House, so much for parables, and perhaps so much, too, for nonprofessionals mucking about in the alleviation of psychological dis-ease or the remediation of psychopathological disorder.

Perhaps inspecting a single, explosive example of one of the newer forms of psychotherapeutic intervention was doomed from the outset as a forlorn enterprise. Better, if we wish a flavor of disorder-remedying or dis-ease-alleviating at their highest levels in our humanely caring society, to look to the works and workings of the doctoral-level professionals, especially since, by now, most of them have themselves become members of a maturing "liberal establishment."

To understand the specifics of the workings of psychotherapy in its customary level of professional practice, we might inspect the speculative and a priori models of mental health and illness (psychopathology and its obverse) advanced by the principal proponents of the several schools of psychotherapeutic practice. But that exercise proves less instructive than inspection of the operational criteria these spokespersons specify in respect of when it is appropriate to terminate professional psychotherapeutic treatment. In this manner, we might discern clearly the end-points in the treatment process, then look backwards at the specific therapeutic techniques by which the psychopathologically dis-eased who presents himself or herself for professional treatment is professionally assisted toward that end-point.

The third editon of Lewis Wolberg's encyclopedic *The Technique of Psychotherapy* consumes 1,343 pages in two volumes. Wolberg, an eminent psychoanalyst and dean emeritus of the prestigious Post-Graduate Center for Mental Health in New York, devotes 15 chapters and 128 pages (more than 10 percent of text matter, exclusive of references and indices) to the initial phases of psychotherapeutic treatment for psychopathological conditions, primarily to the dynamics of the initial interview—and 16 pages (1 percent of the total) to the process of termination. In his discussion of the criteria for termination of psychotherapeutic treatment, Wolberg sets it forth that termination is appropriate (with emphasis added) ''when the patient has achieved optimal functioning *within the limit of his financial circumstances*''[1]—it is too embarrassing to quote further.

Nor is the phenomenon singular. For two decades, in one or another course for doctoral candidates in professional psychology, it has been my practice to require students to prepare a paper on this topic: ''The concept of the mentally healthy person as inferred from the criteria for the termination of psychotherapy enunciated by—fill in the name of your favorite theorist in psychotherapy.''

After they have been at the task for some while, students hesitate not in the least to denounce yours truly as sadistic, nor to characterize the assignment as constituting cruel and unusual punishment. Their experience of the task proves virtually uniform. With very few exceptions, they find in the writings of their favorite theorists no statement of the criteria for termination, but they locate abundant, closely reasoned, conceptually elegant statements of an a priori and speculative nature about when to commence, and these across theories of psychotherapy founded on widely divergent conceptual bases; they encounter many statements and many thousands of words on how to go about the initial interview, but they rarely discover anything at all about conducting the final interview—or, more pertinently, about *when* it should be conducted, in consequence of what operational approximation to their favorite theorist's a priori conceptual model of mental health.
    A curious state of affairs: We know, or believe we know, quite a lot

about when to begin, but precious little about when, where, or why to end.

How does it happen that our operational criteria for termination are unclear?

Substantially before our humanely caring society commissioned cadres of poorly-trained or untrained people-helpers to provide those questionable new forms of disorder-remedying and/or dis-ease-alleviating, the well-known clinician Victor Raimy defined psychotherapy as "an undefined technique applied to unspecified problems with unpredictable outcomes."[2]

At this distance, and especially given a range of mental health services far broader than the narrow-gauge of Raimy's time, is it the case that the techniques used in the panoply of professional people-helping services in our humanely caring society are still variable and nonspecific? Are the outcomes of those new forms of people-helping still so unpredictable as Raimy seemed to believe? And is it the case that our outcomes are unpredictable *because* our techniques are variable and nonspecific? Or is it rather that our techniques are variable and nonspecific because we share no common perception of what their outcomes should or ought to be? Do we use dissimilar methods to reach common end-points—or are our methods dissimilar because our intended end-points are dissimilar as well?

At only a slight risk of caricature, one might argue precisely the latter case.

Wolberg's inartful remark, the persistent inability to locate clear, concise, operationally useful criteria for termination of professional psychotherapy in the pronouncements of the leaders of the principal schools in psychotherapeutic theory and practice, taken together with the earthy tones of the Sunrise House experience *and* a body of more systematic evidence seem to portray contemporary professional psychotherapy in rather a state of general disarray. The body of both scientific and anecdotal evidence seems to indicate that:

• The evidence is not clear that any form of professional psychotherapeutic intervention is more than marginally effective in the treatment of psychopathological disorder and dis-ease among either adults or children; thus, the relief of psychopathology is *not* dependably associated with psychotherapeutic treatment.[3] In the absence of convincing evidence on the efficacy of psychotherapy to relieve that pathology that is its special focus, even so distinguished a card-carrying doctoral-level psychologist as Bernard Rimland, a winner of the American Psychological Foundation's Research Medal, has expressed ethical reservations about continuing the practice of a method of intervention in human affairs with so poor a track record. Though he may overstate the case for polemical purposes, Rimland asserts:

> Negative results have issued from virtually all of the multitude of controlled studies which have evaluated psychotherapy. Persons given intensive and prolonged treatment have been found to be not one whit better off than matched control groups given no treatment over the same time interval. Many doubts have been expressed, both privately and publicly, concerning the ethics of continuing the practice of psychotherapy in view of the dramatically consistent negative findings.[4]

• The evidence mounts that professional psychotherapeutic treatment is associated with negative rather than positive results for some portion of the clients or patients to whom it is applied; thus, some patients appear to deterioriate as a result of psychotherapeutic treatment.[5] A number of inventive psychotherapists propose that this "deterioration effect" masks important positive effects observable in the patient's behavior while he or she remains under regular "therapeutic surveillance," an intriguing proposition that surely accords with Illich's portrayal of a system of lifelong clienthood. Others propose that the evidence has been read too hastily, that the finding that the client has deteriorated with respect to the psychopathological condition for which he or she initially sought (or was forced into) professional treatment may mask important gains in other spheres of life activity not customarily measured in research investigations of therapeutic outcome, a position which surely resonates to images of conjuring.

• No profession-wide criteria obtain for the termination of psychotherapeutic treatment of psychopathological disorder in general and dis-ease in particular. Such criteria for termination as have been propounded, implied, or in some cases concealed, by the proponents of the several schools of theory and practice remain vague, ambiguous, and lack the specificity associated with criteria for termination of the treatment of physical pathology;[6] these ambiguities reveal the lack of clarity, no less than lack of profession-wide unanimity, in the very concepts of psychological pathology and non-pathology, of mental illness and health. In far less elevated language: Unless you know where you're going, it's difficult to know when you get there.

- In the vacuum created by lack of serviceable profession-wide definitions of psychopathology and its obverse, of mental illness and health, the sometimes highly idiosyncratic conceptions advocated by the leading proponents of the several schools have filled a conceptual breach.[7] These conceptions reveal far more disparity than similarity and are further heavily value-laden; they reflect not only the values of the theorists and schools by whom they have been advocated but also those of some portion of the society at large. Because of wide interest in psychopathological dis-ease in particular and in the processes of dis-ease-alleviating among members of the society, fostered by the weekly fare of the entertainment media, the main currents of thought in the leading schools of contemporary psychotherapy have become part of the general cultural consciousness; thus, the sometimes idiosyncratic concepts of mental health and illness espoused by these schools also *shape* the values of some portion of the society, and likely a particularly well-educated and sensitive portion at that.

If it be the case that the divergent conceptions of psychological health proposed by the several diverging schools present the end-points toward which professional psychotherapists of differing stripe direct their efforts, it surely seems that our methods for treatment are variable and nonspecific precisely because the end-points posited as targets by the several schools are not only not identical but barely similar. So, openly risking accusations of caricature, let's compare and contrast end-points and methods.

First, the *psychoanalytic* school—and here we might include the handful of unreconstructed Freudians along with the many neo-Freudians, ego-analysts, and others whose system of treatment rests on the assumption of a mental apparatus consisting of id, ego, and superego, on the positing of unconscious drives and motivations, and on the basic premise that psychopathological conditions stem either from failures in the process of psychosexual development or from failures in the ego to control the hostile, uncivilized impulses of the id.

The analysts aim at uncovering unconscious motivation, so that impulses can be controlled rationally, and at admitting into consciousness traumatic past life events, so that the unconscious memory of such events does not negatively influence present and future behavior. How, then, could we describe the mentally healthy person from the perspective of the analysts? That person is *aware* of his or her *impulses* and *drives*; he or she is supremely rational; while he or she is aware of his or her impulses and drives, he or she discharges those impulses and drives into behavior only after they have been socialized through the process of cognitive mediation.[8] To reach this point may require, in orthodox psychoanalysis, a period of five years of three sessions weekly.

Consider now the school variously identified as *existential*, "phenomenological," or "humanistic." Here we might include those who practice the client-centered therapy of Carl Rogers, the Gestalt therapy of Fritz Perls, or one of the many variants of encounter or self-actualization therapy.

Among the members of this school, or perhaps set of related schools, we shall not often encounter the traditional term "mental health;" instead, we will find terms like "fully functioning person," "self-actualized person," even "beautiful person." What are the characteristics of the persons thus variously denominated? They *live existentially*—that is, they are attuned primarily to the here-and-now; they display *the courage to be*—that is, they are aware of what the analysts might call their impulses and inclinations, but they are willing to act upon them; and they are, in Rogers' words, not bound by their pasts, so they possess *the courage to become*. Spontaneity and existentiality are their principal attributes.[9] In the heyday of Esalen, Aureon, and all that, the optimal fully functioning, self-actualized, "beautiful" person could at least implicitly be operationally defined as one who showed a willingness to abrogate his or her responsibilities (responsibilities that were, to be sure, accepted when he or she was not free and lacked the courage to be and to become and which therefore no longer bound one), in order to live fully, spontaneously, in the here-and-now. There was a time when the term "hedonist" might have been held to apply.

Turn now to the school of *behavior therapy*. Members of this school hold more modest aims than either the analysts or the existentialists; they define their task in treatment as teaching the patient to "unlearn" a behavior that is either maladaptive or undesirable, ineffective either in relation to the patient's goals or inappropriate from the perspective of society. Treatment proceeds either by way of the extinction of the "target" behavior, often by means of learning a new, more appropriate or more acceptable behavior or a behavior incompatible with the target behavior, or by way of learning new behaviors that represent net additions to the client's "behavioral repertoire" for use under the appropriate stimulus contingencies.

The conception of the human person held by this school seems to be that the person is a bundle or aggregate of learned responses; terms like "scope," "depth," or "integration" are generally not part of the behaviorists' lexicon. What, then, is the mentally healthy person for a behaviorist? He or she is a person *free from maladaptive behaviors* who has been *conditioned to emit only effective or appropriate behaviors* governed by precise sets of external contingencies.[10] He/she is, then, essentially passive and reactive—surely not aware of his/her impulses, nor free to be and to become.

What can be said of the overlap between the conceptualizations, broadly sketched here, of the mentally healthy person held by the principal schools in contemporary psychotherapy?

It would appear that the patient who has been *successfully* therapized by a behaviorist might be seen as one who lacks the capacities or habits of reflection and insight that are central, though in very different ways, to the processes of treatment in the psychoanalytic and existential-phenomenological schools. It is perhaps not too much to posit that such a patient—one who behaves, however effectively or appropriately, reflexively and with little thought might be regarded as a likely candidate to *begin* psychoanalytic or existential treatment. And the patient who has been successfully therapized by the existentialist—who has achieved that state in which he or she is not only aware of his or her feelings and impulses but is not afraid to act upon them, the devil take the consequences—might be considered by the analyst as clearly in need of treatment, for he or she lacks the capacity to control impulses through the cognitive mediation of the ego which is the end-point of analytic treatment.

So, if the end-point in treatment for one school can be seen, even at the risk of caricature, to coincide with the beginning-point in treatment for another, the evidence is strong that our treatment methods are variable and nonspecific because we are trying to reach different end-points, each highly idiosyncratic, by equally idiosyncratic routes.

But that leaves largely unanswered the pivotal and vexing questions: What is mental health, and by whose definition? What is psychopathology, and how do you know when it's "cured?" Who defines what therapeutic results are positive and which negative, and what values undergird that definition? Are we to be left with no more than idiosyncracy compounded with self-interest and transformed into creed?

In his review of the then-published studies on how the values of the therapist affect the patient, Walter Doyle concluded: "The evidence indicates a tendency in psychotherapeutic relationships for the client to move in the direction of the therapist in moral values, personality and character structure, and even verbal behavior." Since these effects seem to obtain even when therapists "take great precautions to avoid influencing their patients' values in any way, it may be that the therapist communicates his values to the patient in many unintended, subtle ways, even when trying to avoid doing so." But, most pertinently: "Clients do not become similar to some central, broadly shared criterion of moral value; *they simply grow more like their particular therapists*."[11]

Notes

1. Lewis R. Wolberg, *The Technique of Psychotherapy*, 3d ed. (New York: Grune & Stratton, 1977), pp. 11-17.
2. Victor A. Raimy, *Training in Clinical Psychology* (New York: Prentice Hall, 1950), p. 93. In full context, the oft-quoted remark is less iconoclastic: "A somewhat facetious assessment of the present situation [in the training of clinical psychologists] was given by one Conference participant who suggested, "Psychotherapy is an undefined technique applied to unspecified problems with unpredictable outcomes. For this technique we recommend rigorous training."
3. The evidence that supports this proposition is found in these sources: Hans J. Eysenck, *The Effects of Psychotherapy* (New York: International Science Press, 1966); Allen E. Bergin, "The Evaluation of Therapeutic Outcomes," pp. 217-70, and Eugene E. Levitt, "Research on Psychotherapy with Children," pp. 474-94, both in Allen E. Bergin and Sol L. Garfield, eds., *Handbook of Psychotherapy and Behavior Change* (New York: Wiley, 1971); Allen E. Bergin and Michael J. Lambert, "The Evaluation of Therapeutic Outcomes," pp. 139-90, and Curtis L. Barrett, I. Edward Hampe, and Lovick Miller, "Research on Psychotherapy with Children," pp. 437-90, both in Sol L. Garfield and Allen E. Bergin, eds., *Handbook of Psychotherapy and Behavior*

Change, 2d ed. (New York: Wiley, 1978); Mary Lee Smith, Gene V. Glass, and Thomas I. Miller, *The Benefits of Psychotherapy* (Baltimore: Johns Hopkins University Press, 1980); S.J. Rachman and G.T. Wilson, *The Effects of Psychological Therapy*, 2d ed. (Oxford: Pergammon, 1980).

4. Bernard Rimland, "Psychiatry Overextended," *Science* 154 (1966), 1935.

5. This proposition rests initially on two analyses by Allen E. Bergin: "The Effects of Psychotherapy: Negative Results Revisited," *Journal of Counseling Psychology* 10 (1963), 244-50; "Psychotherapy Can Be Dangerous—Sometimes," *Psychology Today* (November 1975), pp. 96-100, 104. In addition to these brief treatments, a more systematic analysis is included in the section on "Deterioriation Effects Revisited" in Bergin and Lambert, "The Evaluation of Therapeutic Outcomes" (note 3). In his 1975 report, Bergin reviewed some 30 studies of the outcomes of psychotherapy which, in the aggregate, suggest that about 10 percent of those who are "treated" deteriorate thereafter—a proportion approximately double that found among "otherwise similar" control subjects in these studies who were said to evince the same sort of disorders but received no treatment; the implication seems to be that about twice as many subjects who receive psychotherapy get worse thereafter when compared to those who need but do not get psychotherapeutic treatment. In their more voluminous and precise review, Bergin and Lambert are more cautious, observing only that deterioration in psychological functioning is now recognized as a sufficiently dependable phenomenon to become a variable of interest in research on psychotherapeutic outcome. An important conceptual approach to the interpretation of both positive outcomes and deterioration effects has been formulated by Hans H. Strupp and Suzanne W. Hadley ("A Tripartite Model of Mental Health and Therapeutic Outcomes with Special Reference to Negative Effects in Psychotherapy," *American Psychologist* 32 [1977], 187-96), who propose that outcomes should be judged not merely from the intrapsychic and interpersonal perspective of the patient but also from the perspectives of society and the mental health profession; in their system, a particular outcome could be judged negative from one perspective but positive from another—e.g., the niggling guilt experienced by an advocate of man-boy love grows during therapy to incapacitating remorse. The present writer has opined elsewhere that, at least among dually deviant criminal offenders, it may be that a "temporary benefit" accrues to some clients while they remain in treatment as a consequence of the therapist's implicit function as critic and monitor of their behavior and that deterioration is observed once such "therapeutic surveillance," often ordered by a court as a condition of probation or parole, is no longer present as a factor in the determination of their behavior; the theme is expanded in "Currently Discernible Trends and the Contours of Parole Policy and Practice in 1990," *Offender Rehabilitation* 4 (1980), 153-61.

6. Among many others, Rachman and Wilson, *The Effects of Psychological Therapy*, p. 258, have called for "greater directness, specificity, and . . . the establishment of explicit treatment goals" to counter the situation described here.

7. In her *Current Concepts of Positive Mental Health* (New York: Basic Books, 1958), the report of the White House Conference devoted to the topic, Marie Jahoda treats the lack of a commonly accepted definition at some length, complains of "the elusiveness of the concept of mental health," observes that "there exists no operationally useful description," and finally offers a curiously circular and nonspecific five-part definition of her own—but one that is, nonetheless, held as "a contemporary ideal model of mental health or normality" (Peter E. Nathan and Sandra L. Harris, *Psychopathology and Society* [New York: McGraw-Hill, 1975], p. 8).

8. The most useful sources: Otto Fenichel, *The Psychoanalytic Theory of Neurosis* (New York: Norton, 1945); Franz Alexander, *Fundamentals of Psychoanalysis* (New York: Norton, 1948); Herman Nunberg, *Principles of Psychoanalysis* (New York: International Universities Press, 1955); Isidor Chein, *The Science of Behavior and the Image of Man* (New York: Basic Books, 1972); Charles Brenner, *An Elementary Textbook of Psychoanalysis* (New York: International Univiersities Press, 1973); David P. Ausubel and Daniel Kirk, *Ego Psychology and Mental Disorder* (New York: Grune & Stratton, 1977). A remarkable bit of whimsy by Fred Schectman ("Conventional and Contemporary Approaches to Psychotherapy: Freud Meets Skinner, Janov, and Others," *American Psychologist* 32 [1977], 197-204), in the form of an imaginary dialogue between nondoctrinnaire protagonists, is instructive.

9. The principal sources: Carl R. Rogers, *Counseling and Psychotherapy* (Boston: Houghton Mifflin, 1942); *Client-Centered Therapy* (Boston: Houghton Mifflin, 1951); *On Becoming a Person* (Boston: Houghton Mifflin, 1961); "The Concept of the Fully Functioning Person," *Psychotherapy* 1 (1963), 17-26. See also Abraham H. Maslow, *Motivation and Personality*, 2d ed., (New York: Harper & Row, 1970), esp. pp. 241-80; Joseph Hart and Thomas Tomlinson, eds., *New Directions in Client-Centered Therapy* (Boston: Houghton Mifflin, 1970); Rollo May, *The Courage to Create* (New York: W.W. Norton, 1975).

10. The most useful sources: Joseph Wolpe and Arnold Lazarus, *Behavior Therapy Techniques* (New York: Pergamon, 1966); Joseph Wolpe, *The Practice of Behavior Therapy* (New York: Pergamon, 1969); Michael R. Goldfried and Gerald C. Davison, *Clinical Behavior Therapy* (New York: Holt, Rinehart, Winston, 1976). Less doctrinnaire views are found in Arnold A. Lazarus, *Multimodal Behavior Therapy* (New York: Springer, 1976); G. Terence Wilson and Daniel O'Leary, *Principles of Behavior Therapy* (Englewood Cliffs, N.J.: Prentice-Hall, 1980); Lazarus, *The Practice of Multimodal Therapy* (New York: McGraw-Hill, 1981). Lazarus' "Has Behavior Therapy Outlived Its Usefulness?"

(*American Psychologist* 32, [1977], pp. 550-54) is most informative as an "insider's" criticism. Fred Schectman ("Operant Conditioning and Psychoanalysis," in Judd Marmor and Sherwyn Woods, eds., *The Interface between the Psychodynamic and Behavioral Therapies* [New York: Plenum, 1980], pp. 95-103), in terms reminiscent of the debates of the mid-1960s that followed publication of B.F. Skinner's *Beyond Freedom and Dignity*, characterizes the view of the person implicit in behavior therapy as "a repugnant framework which conceptualizes Man as an aggregate of habits or group of behaviors to be shaped and manipulated." In contrast, Robert L. Woolfolk and Frank C. Richardson ("Behavior Therapy and the Ideology of Modernity," *American Psychologist* 32 [1984], 777-86) argue the essential humanism of behavior therapy, characterizing it as a "reform movement that sought to hold the feet of dogmatic therapeutic creeds to the fire of empirical test, to challenge irrational authority, and to unleash human capacities for exploration, achievement, and self-determination."

11. Walter L. Doyle, "The Effects of Counselor Values: Theory and Research," in *Readings for Catholic Counselors*, 3d ed. (Milwaukee: National Catholic Guidance Conference, 1966), pp. 116-24. In a roughly parallel formulation, social critic John McKnight ("Professionalized Service and Disabling Help," in *The Disabling Professions* [London: Marion Boyars, 1978], pp. 69-91) has it that: "Modernized professional services increasingly communicate the value of being an effective client as the proof of the system's efficacy. We will have reached the apogee of the modernized service society when the professionals can say to the citizen: We are the solution to your problem. We know what problems you have. You can't understand the problem or the solution. Only we can decide whether the solution has dealt with your problems ... service systems are training citizens to understand that their satisfaction is [to be] derived from being effective clients rather than people whose problems are solved." He expands the theme in *The Mask of Love: Professional Care in the Service Economy* (London: Marion Boyars, 1982).

12
Beyond Laing and Szasz

Witty aphorisms, unsubtle ironies, shards, fragments, glimpses, glances. Beyond the cynicism and the sarcasm, however well-intellectualized, will we find substance, a gestalt, a coherent and intelligible pattern? Or have we merely been entertained?

The *that* of it has been implied, if not always directly explicated:

Deviance is a property conferred upon one's behavior by others who find it embarrassing or irritating. Whatever it denotes, psychological dis-ease connotes a subjective experience; but it is entirely plausible that such subjective discomfort might arise because others, particularly those who enjoy a societal status that empowers them to make such judgments, find your behavior embarrassing or irritating—and tell you so.

Psychological health represents the dominance of positive adaptations to the psychosocial environment over negative adaptations to that environment—including adaptations to the people who have defined your behavior as deviant, but, wearing the mask of love, are willing to provide the care you need and to pronounce you "cured" when you become more like them.

And on and on, until we shall have become a society comprised of a deviant majority and its keepers.

The *why* of it becomes yet more mystically speculative.

64

Early on, it was posited that those values any society holds most tenaciously are those essential to its continued existence, for it is the first obligation of any society is to perpetuate itself. And it was similarly posited that these essential values of a society will be exhibited in the structure of the formal institutions which that society establishes to regulate and to perpetuate itself.

It would seem to follow that any society must also establish norms for what it means to be a "good" member of that society and what it means to be a "bad" member, to provide operational definitions of *success* and *failure* according to the normative values of that society. And the conception of the "good life" held by any society will reflect and conform to those norms and definitions.

It would seem also to follow that the need for visible examples of success and failure corresponding to those operational definitions increases when the existence of that society appears to be threatened, whether internally or externally—that is, at any point at which a society is called upon to relocate its boundaries.

Thus, a society which regards itself as sacred, as chosen for direct communication with its gods, needs for its continuity visible examples of the special favor of its gods and of their displeasure—that is, of sanctity and damnation. And similarly:

- A competitive society requires visible examples of successful and unsuccessful competitiveness.
- A society based on an economic system that deliberately limits the production of goods for the benefit of those whose control the means of production requires visible examples of the amassing, and the failure to amass, the means and the fruits of production.
- A society based on an economic system that pre-supposes free market conditions and thus presupposes that superior products will survive, that inferior products will eclipse—a society that presupposes social and economic Darwinism—requires visible examples of the fittest and the least fit among producers and consumers.
- A society that regards itself as egalitarian requires visible examples that whatever it regards as the good life is equally available to all its members.
- A society that regards itself as libertarian requires visible examples that its members may choose freely to pursue whatever it regards as the good life—or choose otherwise, but freely.

But societies are rarely governed at their central core by a discrete, un-contaminated set of essential values. Rather, there are blends, mixtures, emulsions; one or another set of values may predominate, but there are trace elements of other value-sets.

Thus, a society that is both based on a free market economy *and* regards itself as egalitarian will require visible examples of the fruits of the competitive pursuit of whatever it regards as the good life, given a level of opportunity that has been putatively equalized among its members.

A society that both regards itself as egalitarian and libertarian will require visible examples of the free choice of the pursuit of the good life, given conditions in which the level of opportunity for free choice has been putatively equalized among its members.

And a society that sees itself as both sacred and libertarian will require visible examples of the pursuit of sanctity, given conditions in which free choice is putatively available to its members.

Many other cross-breaks are possible, even when we contrast these sets of essential societal values with each other only two at a time; when we contrast three, four, or more at a time, the possibilities expand geometrically, and the metaphysical imagination reels.

Upon such premises, it becomes coherent that a society which deifies its leaders, as did ancient Egypt, or canonizes its exemplary members, as did medieval Europe, must also provide visible examples of those who are damned. And it is ever the case that one highly visible, convenient, ready-to-hand group of candidates for damnation are, understandably enough, those whose behavior is found to be embarrassing, irritating, disaccommodating, those whose behavior is not otherwise explicable according to the cognitive constructs available to the members of a sacred society. Thus, it was culturally imperative in ancient Egypt and in medieval Europe to equate discernible psychopathology no less than psychological dis-ease with damnation. And when cognitive constructs capable of explaining behavioral deviance in terms other than damnation intrude, it is culturally imperative that a sacred society proscribe those constructs, for they too threaten that society's existence. Thus, the suppression of "Arab" medicine, which was not Moslem in origin at all, but no more than the renascence of the naturalistic medicine of Greece and Rome.

In societies which practice human sacrifice, it is typical that the elected victim is a representative of the noblest and the best—indeed, often a prince or princess of the royal blood—for only the noblest and the best will appease powerful gods.

Anthropological eons later, then, it is required that Richard Cory become suicidally depressed—so that the townspeople will take the bread more gladly and curse the absent meat less vehemently.

In a society which prizes the *choice* of goodness over goodness itself, Alex could not be tolerated—not because he failed to choose goodness, but because he proved incapable of choice. But the correctional rehabilitationists who rendered him incapable of choosing evil were no more tolerable than he—witness *Wyatt v. Hardin*.

In a society which prides itself that it has institutionalized humanely the act of caring, we make mental health services widely available to our members through a panoply of services and providers. But we also arrange a set of circumstances that ensure that those of us most in need of those services are provided only a substandard variety.

There is, as ever, another member in the equation.

What of those who experience themselves as psychologically diseased, who perceive their behavior as dis-accommodating to others? To what do they attribute their dis-ease?

Some of their number, and perhaps more than merely some, internalize their society's complex metaphysics of psychopathology. Thus, millenia before Scheff's researches or Illich's scorching insights, in pantheistic Athens in the second century before Christ, Plutarch describes a citizen who "looks on himself as a man whom the gods hate and pursue with their anger," who "dares not employ any means of averting or remedying the evil, lest he be found fighting against the gods." Instead, "The physician and the consoling friend are driven away," and he is filled with self-abnegation: "Leave me . . . me, the impious, the accursed, hated of the gods, to suffer my punishment." And that self-abnegation is expressed behaviorally in ways that clearly provide visible examples of damnation: "He sits out of doors, wrapped in sackcloth; he rolls himself, naked, in the dirt confessing . . . this sin and that. He has gone some way or another that the Divine Being did not approve of.''[1]

How readily Plutarch's subject might have welcomed the medieval exorcist, bell, candle, Witches' Hammer, and *promise of redemption* in hand—doubtless as readily as a Billy Carter, in a society whose conception of psychopathology may be vastly different but which obeys the same metaphysical principles of societal deviance and its regulation, elected, whether with or without political prompting, both to identify himself as dis-eased and to yield himself to the ministrations of contemporary successors to the exorcists, to those who hold both the promise and the key to redemption.

The values of a competitive libertarian society based on a free market economy apply as well to the psychotherapy enterprise as a social institution. Thus, we have not only been permitted but encouraged to develop competing systems, however variable and nonspecific; let only the fittest survive; and all our well-intentioned efforts have yielded such disappointing results because, had we learned to treat the psychopathologically dis-eased more effectively, we might have stemmed the supply of visible examples of failure our society absolutely requires for its continued existence. How else account for such lack of clarity in the criteria for termination of treatment that competing schools in professional psychotherapy have chosen not merely different routes to similar end-points, but substantially different end-points as well?

Thus, it is proposed, essentially the same societal forces engender psychological disorder and dis-ease, enlist armies of professional and paraprofessional disorder-remediators and dis-ease-alleviators, and encourage ambiguity, inefficiency, and inefficacy in the remediating and alleviating enterprises; and, like the other institutions society establishes to regulate itself, contemporary psychotherapy also obeys categorical social imperatives.

In our mutually interactive responses to those inexorable social imperatives—whether we are the psychopathology definers, those who are identified by others as psychopathologically disordered or by ourselves as psychologically dis-eased; whether we are the disorder remediators or the dis-ease-alleviators, or merely the beneficiaries of the efficient exercise of these societally prescribed functions who are enabled by that very efficiency to curse the absent meat less vehemently and accept the bread more gladly—we fulfill roles vital to the maintenance of a society in which visible, publicly identifiable deviance is a necessity.

Note

1. Cited by Zilborg and Henry, *The Medical Man and the Witch during the Renaissance*, p. 67. One can rather readily conceive a system of psychological intervention in self- (rather than other-) defined problems in living free from diagnostic categories which imply the presence of psychopathology, in which the appropriate "treatment" might be modeled after teaching rather than healing, and in which the agents for such "treatment" might be fellow citizens who have mastered certain techniques useful in such intervention but hold no advanced degrees and collect no third-party-reimbursed medical fees; but that system is another topic for another time and place; and whether such a system would be called psychotherapy or, following Schofield, only dependable friendship remains a question not likely to be raised in spirited debate in the professional community.

References

Achenbach, Thomas M. "What Is Child Psychiatric Epidemiology the Epidemiology Of?" In Felton Earls, ed., *Psychosocial Epidemiology: Studies of Children*. New York: Neale Watson Academic, 1980.

Adams, Henry. "Mental Illness or Interpersonal Behavior?" *American Psychologist* 19 (1964), 191-97.

Alexander, Franz. *Fundamentals of Psychoanalysis*. New York: Norton, 1948.

————, and Sheldon T. Selesnick. *The History of Psychiatry: An Evaluation of Psychiatric Thought and Practice*. New York: Harper & Row, 1966.

American Friends Service Committee. *Struggle for Justice*. New York: Hill & Wang, 1971.

American Psychiatric Association. *Diagnostic and Statistical Manual of Mental Disorders*, 3d ed. Washington: The Association, 1980.

Ausubel, David P., and Daniel Kirk. *Ego Psychology and Mental Disorder*. New York: Grune & Stratton, 1977.

Bandler, Richard, and John Grinder. *The Structure of Magic*. Palo Alto: Science & Behavior Books, 1975.

Bazelon, David L. "Psychologists in Corrections: Are They Doing Good for the Offender or Well for Themselves?" In Stanley Brodsky, ed., *Psychologists in the Criminal Justice System*. Urbana: University of Illinois Press, 1973.

Bergin, Allen E. "The Effects of Psychotherapy: Negative Results Revisited," *Journal of Counseling Psychology* 10 (1963), 244-50.

————. "Psychotherapy Can Be Dangerous—Sometimes," *Psychology Today*, (November 1975), 96-100, 104.

70

————, and Sol L. Garfield, eds. *Handbook of Psychotherapy and Behavior Change*. New York: Wiley, 1971.

Brenner, Charles. *An Elementary Textbook of Psychoanalysis*. New York: International Univiersities Press, 1973.

Bromberg, Walter. *The Mind of Man: A History of Psychotherapy and Psychoanalysis*. New York: Harper & Row, 1963.

————. *From Shaman to Psychotherapist: A History of the Treatment of Mental Illness*. Chicago: Henry Regenry, 1975.

Burckhardt, Jacob. *The Civilization of the Renaissance in Italy*. New York: Harper, 1958.

Burgess, Anthony. *A Clockwork Orange*. New York: Norton, 1963.

Burr, George L. *Translations and Reprints from the Original Sources of European History*. Philadelphia: University of Pennsylvania Press, 1897.

Campbell, Donald. *Arabian Medicine and Its Influence In the Middle Ages*. London: Kegan, Paul, French, Trubner, 1926.

Chein, Isidor. *The Science of Behavior and the Image of Man*. New York: Basic Books, 1972.

Clausen, John A. "Mental Disorders." In Robert K. Merton and Robert Nisbet, eds., *Contemporary Social Problems*. New York: Harcourt, Brace, Jovanovich, 1971.

————, Nancy G. Pfeffer, and Carol L. Huffine. "Help-Seeking in Severe Mental Illness." In David Mechanic, ed., *Symptoms, Illness Behavior, and Help-Seeking*. New York: Prodist/Neale Watson, 1982.

Dohrenwend, Bruce P., and Barbara Snell Dohrenwend. *Social Status and Psychological Disorders*. New York: Wiley, 1969.

Doyle, Walter L. "The Effects of Counselor Values: Theory and Research." In *Readings for Catholic Counselors*, 3d ed. Milwaukee: National Catholic Guidance Conference, 1966.

Draper, John William. *History of the Conflict between Religion and Science*. New York: D. Appleton, 1875.

Erikson, Kai T. *Wayward Puritans: A Study in the Sociology of Deviance*. New York: Wiley, 1966.

Eysenck, Hans J. *The Effects of Psychotherapy*. New York: International Science Press, 1966.

————. *Crime and Personality*. London: Routledge & Kegan Paul, 1977.

Faris, Robert E.L., and H. Warren Dunham. *Mental Disorders in Urban Areas*. Chicago: University of Chicago Press, 1939.

Fenichel, Otto. *The Psychoanalytic Theory of Neurosis*. New York: Norton, 1945.

Foucault, Michel. *Madness and Civilization: A History of Insanity in the Age of Reason*. New York: Random House, 1965.

————. *Discipline and Punish: The Birth of the Prison*. New York: Pantheon, 1978.

Garfield, Sol L., and Allen E. Bergin, eds. *Handbook of Psychotherapy and Behavior Change*, 2d ed. New York: Wiley, 1978.

Garrison, Fielding. *An Introduction to the History of Medicine*. Philadelphia: W.B. Saunders, 1924.

Ghalioungui, Paul. *The House of Life: Magic and Medical Science in Ancient Egypt*. Amsterdam: Israel, 1973.

Golann, Stuart, and William J. Fremouw, eds. *The Right to Treatment for Mental Patients*. New York: Irvington, 1976.

Goldfried, Michael R., and Gerald C. Davison. *Clinical Behavior Therapy*. New York: Holt, Rinehart, Winston, 1976.

Goldhamer, Herbert, and Andrew W. Marshall. *Psychosis and Civilization*. Glencoe, IL: Free Press, 1949.

Gonzalez, Justo L. *A History of Christian Thought from Augustine to the Eve of the Reformation*. Nashville: Abingdon Press, 1971.

Goshen, Charles E. *A Documentary History of Psychiatry: A Source Book on Historical Principles*. New York: Philosophical Library, 1967.

Haggard, Howard W. *Devils, Drugs, and Doctors*. New York: Blue Ribbon, 1929.

————. *Mystery, Magic, and Medicine*. Garden City, N.Y.: Doubleday, 1933.

Hart, Joseph, and Thomas Tomlinson, eds. *New Directions in Client-Centered Therapy*. Boston: Houghton-Mifflin, 1970.

Hollingshead, August de B., and Frederick C. Redlich. *Social Class and Mental Illness*. New York: Wiley, 1958.

Huxley, Aldous. *The Devils of Loudon*. New York: Harper & Bros., 1953.

Ilfeld, Frederic W., Jr. "Psychological Status of Community Residents along Major Demographic Dimensions," *Archives of General Psychiatry* 35 (1978), 716-24.

Illich, Ivan. *Medical Nemesis: The Expropriation of Health*. London: Calder & Boyars, 1975.

————. *Toward a History of Needs*. New York: Pantheon, 1978.

Jahoda, Marie. *Current Concepts of Positive Mental Health*. New York: Basic Books, 1958.

Kirsch, Irving. "Demonology and the Rise of Science: An Example of the Misperception of Historial Data," *Journal of the History of the Behavioral Sciences* 14 (1978), 149-57.

Korchin, Sheldon. *Modern Clinical Psychology*. New York: Basic Books, 1976.

Kramer, Morton. *Psychiatric Services and the Changing Institutional Scene, 1950-85*. Rockville, MD: National Institute of Mental Health, 1977.

Kuhner, Hans. *The Encylopedia of the Papacy*. New York: Philosophical Library, 1958.

Laing, Ronald D. *The Divided Self*. London: Tavistock, 1960.

———. *Self and Others*. New York: Pantheon, 1969.

———. *The Politics of the Family*. New York: Pantheon, 1971.

———. *Knots*. New York: Pantheon, 1971.

———. *Do You Love Me?* New York: Pantheon, 1976.

Lazarus, Arnold A. *Multimodal Behavior Therapy*. New York: Springer, 1976.

———. "Has Behavior Therapy Outlived Its Usefulness?" *American Psychologist* 32 (1977), 550-54.

———. *The Practice of Multimodal Therapy*. New York: McGraw-Hill, 1981.

Leighton, Dorothea C., Alexander H. Leighton, and R.A. Armstrong. "Community Psychiatry in a Rural Area: A Social Psychiatric Approach." In Leopold Bellak, ed., *Handbook of Community Psychiatry*. New York: Grune & Stratton, 1968.

MacKinney, Loren. *Medical Illustrations in Medieval Manuscripts*. Berkeley: University of California Press, 1965.

McKnight, John L. "Professionalized Service and Disabling Help." In Ivan Illich, ed., *The Disabling Professions*. London: Marion Boyars, 1978.

———. *The Mask of Love: Professional Care in the Service Economy*. London: Marion Boyars, 1982.

Mappen, Marc, ed. *Witches and Historians: Interpretations of Salem*. Huntington, NY: Robert E. Krieger, 1980.

Maritain, Jacques. *Three Reformers: Luther–Descartes–Rousseau*. London: Sheed & Ward, 1941.

Martinson, Robert. "California Research at the Crossroads." *Crime and Delinquency* 14 (1976), 189-99.

Maslow, Abraham H. *Motivation and Personality*, 2d ed. New York: Harper & Row, 1970.

May, Rollo. *The Courage to Create*. New York: W.W. Norton, 1975.

Mechanic, David. *Mental Health and Social Policy*. Englewood Cliffs, N.J.: Prentice-Hall, 1980.

Myers, Jerome K., and Bertram H. Roberts. *Family and Class Dynamics in Mental Illness*. New York: Wiley, 1959.

———, and Lee L. Bean. *A Decade Later*. New York: Wiley, 1968.

Nathan, Peter E., and Sandra L. Harris. *Psychopathology and Society*. New York: McGraw-Hill, 1975.

Nunberg, Herman. *Principles of Psychoanalysis*. New York: International Universities Press, 1955.

Opler, Marvin K. *Culture and Social Psychiatry*. New York: Atherton, 1967.

Pallone, Nathaniel J. "Currently Discernible Trends and the Contours of Parole Policy and Practice in 1990," *Offender Rehabilitation* 4 (1980), 153-61.

Plunkett, Richard J., and John E. Gordon. *Epidemiology and Mental Illness*. New York: Basic Books, 1960.

Rachman, S.J., and G.T. Wilson, *The Effects of Psychological Therapy*, 2d ed. Oxford: Pergamon, 1980.

Raimy, Victor A. *Training in Clinical Psychology*. New York: Prentice-Hall, 1950.

Rashdall, Hastings. *The Universities of Europe in the Middle Ages*. Oxford: Clarendon Press, 1936.

Rimland, Bernard. "Psychiatry Overextended," *Science* 154 (1966), 1395.

Robinson, Edward Arlington. *The Children of the Night*. New York: Charles Scribner's Sons, 1905.

Rogers, Carl R. *Counseling and Psychotherapy*. Boston: Houghton Mifflin, 1942.

———. *Client-Centered Therapy*. Boston: Houghton Mifflin, 1951.

———. *On Becoming a Person*. Boston: Houghton Mifflin, 1961.

———. "The Concept of the Fully Functioning Person," *Psychotherapy* 1 (1963), 17-26.

Rosen, George. *Madness in Society*. Chicago: University of Chicago Press, 1968.

Sarbin, Theodore R., and James C. Mancuso. *Schizophrenia: Medical Diagnosis or Moral Verdict?* New York: Pergamon, 1980.

Schectman, Fred. "Conventional and Contemporary Approaches to Psychotherapy: Freud Meets Skinner, Janov, and Others," *American Psychologist* 32 (1977), 197-204.

———. "Operant Conditioning and Psychoanalysis." In Judd Marmor and Sherwyn Woods, eds., *The Interface between the Psychodynamic and Behavioral Therapies*. New York: Plenum, 1980.

Scheff, Thomas J. "The Societal Reaction to Deviance: Ascriptive Elements in the Psychiatric Screening of Mental Patients in a Midwestern State Hospital," *Social Problems* 11 (1964), 401-13.

———. *Being Mentally Ill: A Sociological Theory*. Chicago: Aldine, 1966.

Schofield, William. *Psychotherapy: The Purchase of Friendship*. Englewood Cliffs, N.J.: Prentice-Hall, 1964.

Shannon, Albert Clement. *The Popes and Heresy in the Thirteenth Century*. Villanova, Pa.: Augustinian Press, 1949.

Sigerist, Henry E. *Civilization and Disease*. Ithaca: Cornell University Press, 1945.

Singer, Charles, and Dorothea Singer. "The Origin of the Medical School of Salerno, the First University." In Charles Singer and Henry E. Sigerist, eds., *Essays on the History of Medicine*. Freeport: Books for Libraries Press, 1924.

Smith, Mary Lee, Gene V. Glass, and Thomas I. Miller. *The Benefits of Psychotherapy*. Baltimore: Johns Hopkins University Press, 1980.

Spanos, Nicholas P. "Witchcraft in Histories of Psychiatry: A Critical Analysis and an Alternative Conceptualization," *Psychological Bulletin* 85 (1978), 417-39.

Srole, Leo, Thomas S. Langer, Stanley T. Michael, Marvin K. Opler, and Thomas A.C. Bennie. *Mental Health in the Metropolis*. New York: McGraw-Hill, 1962.

Strupp, Hans H., and Suzanne W. Hadley. "A Tripartite Model of Mental Health and Therapeutic Outcomes with Special Reference to Negative Effects in Psychotherapy," *American Psychologist* 32 (1977), 187-96.

Summers, Montague, ed. *The Malleus Maleficaricum of Heinrich Kramer and James Sprenger*. London: John Rodker, 1928, 1948; New York: Dover, 1971.

Szasz, Thomas S. *The Myth of Mental Illness*. New York: Harper & Row, 1961.

————. *Law, Liberty, and Psychiatry*. New York: Collier, 1968.

————. *The Manufacture of Madness*. New York: Harper & Row: 1970.

————. *Psychiatric Slavery*. New York: Pantheon, 1978.

Tweed, Dan, Mildred Konan, and James W. Longest. *Distribution of Mental Health Manpower in the United States*. College Park: Division of Agriculture and Life Sciences, University of Maryland, 1977.

Weissman, Myrna M., Jerome K. Myers, and Pamela S. Harding. "Psychiatric Disorders in a U.S. Urban Community," *American Journal of Psychiatry* 135 (1978), 459-62.

Wilson, G. Terence, and Daniel O'Leary. *Principles of Behavior Therapy*. Englewood Cliffs, N.J.: Prentice-Hall, 1980.

Wolberg, Lewis R. *The Technique of Psychotherapy*, 3d ed. New York: Grune & Stratton, 1977.

Wolpe, Joseph. *The Practice of Behavior Therapy*. New York: Pergamon, 1969.

————, and Arnold Lazarus. *Behavior Therapy Techniques*. New York: Pergamon, 1966.

Woolfolk, Robert L., and Frank C. Richardson. "Behavior Therapy and the Ideology of Modernity," *American Psychologist* 32 (1984), 777-86.

Zilborg, Gregory. *The Medical Man and the Witch During the Renaissance*. Baltimore: Johns Hopkins University Press, 1935.

————, and George W. Henry. *A History of Medical Psychology*. New York: Norton, 1941.

Index